The Weight of the Wait

SPIRTUAL DEVELOPMENT THROUGH THE JOURNEY TO A PROMISE

The Weight of the Wait
©2021 Aria Gaines
Published by: Aria Gaines

ISBN: 978-0-578-97277-0
Library of Congress number: 2021918701

Edited by: Keyoka Kinzy
Cover and Interior Layout: Write on Promotions

Dedication

Neuma,

I haven't even typed anything, and I am already crying. This one goes to You, Holy Spirit. God, you always deserve the first fruit of all things. I couldn't dedicate this book to anyone but You.

You have walked with me, talked with me, and guided me from the beginning of time. Even as I sit in room 905 typing these words, You have led me to this place (Tallahassee) to be one with You.

This journey has not been easy, but as You spoke to me earlier today, You were with me when I first came here, and You have been with me this weekend. So as I drove around today, I saw many familiar places knowing You were showing them to me, not understanding why.

As I was questioning my time here in this place, I felt You wanted me to remember everything from before because there is about to be a shift. So You said to me, "After this, your life is about to change forever, and I wanted this time with you. Would you have come if I told you it was to spend time with Me? I just wanted you to be with Me. Do you not find value in that?"

Neuma, I do, and I thank You for pushing me to my highest potential. Thank You for just who You are to me at any given moment.

I will love You for eternity,

Your daughter,

Acknowledgments

To my dearest family and friends. I hold you as closely as the thoughts that precede the words on this page, you are a part of me. A part of my victories, my failures, my laughs, my tears, my world. You see the foundation of my faith was built on relationship, and I can definitively say I wouldn't be where I am today without the way each of you have inspired and supported me.

A special thanks to Daddy, Mama, and Ju. You all have played vital roles in the woman I have become, and I'm so blessed God chose you three for me.

Acknowledgments

To my dearest family and friends, I hold you as closely as the thoughts that precede the words on this page, you are a part of me, a part of my violence, my failures, my triumphs, my fears, my world. You see the foundation of my faith was built on relationship, and I can definitively say I wouldn't be where I am today without that. Each of you have inspired and supported me.

A special thanks to Daddy, Muffin and J.J. You all have played vital roles in the woman I have become, and I'm so honored that God chose you three for me.

Preface

I met my husband years before we got married. Not uncommon, right? Well, what if I told you the Lord showed me who he was? Again, that happens; God reveals things to people all the time. How about the fact that I had barely spoken to or seen him before I received the revelation, not to mention I was more than sure he hadn't gotten the same memo? I'm sure you can only imagine the state of confusion I was in with all of that said. All of this and more are crucial pieces of a journey that would change my life forever. Writing this book is undeniably a huge step of faith, and regardless of the overwhelming "what ifs'" I am encouraged to document my experiences.

In my life, dating was always something that took me on a never-ending roller coaster in some way or another. That pattern motivated me to seek change, so I began to put more energy into my relationship with God. I thought that if I focused on Him, I would forget how much I longed to be married. I thought this change would give me something positive and rewarding to focus on. I figured if I tried hard enough to be pleasing to the Lord, then it would happen for me. I thought that if I did everything the church tells you to do as a young Christian single, then my husband would come. I didn't realize that even with my selfish intent, God would still meet me right where I was.

As I grew closer to Christ, I began to see my understanding change from a work-based mindset into a deeper relationship. During that time, the Lord began to reveal things about the man I would marry. He was answering my heart's longing prayer, but it would take some time for me to realize it. To my surprise, I knew the person He was showing me. We met at a collegiate track meet in April of 2011, my junior year in college. Our first encounter was anything but romantic, to say the least; however, that day, he discerned something about my character that, unbeknownst to him, would define the essence of my entire existence.

This book highlights numerous points of my journey as I navigate the voice of God in a world that primarily believes what is perceived physically. There is nothing more complicated than walking with the Lord and trusting something that looks impossible. Yet, even in times of doubt, I am called to remember that God's word never returns to Him void (Isaiah

55:11), and with man, this would be impossible, but with God, all things are possible (Matthew 19:26).

Foreword

Close your eyes. Imagine an early Sunday morning, getting a whiff of a sweet aroma lingering from coffee freshly brewed. Pleased to hear a beep from the coffee pot, you sashay over to the kitchen to pour two cups of perfection. You eagerly return to the living room with anticipation, carefully balancing the hot, medium-dark roast. Before getting ultimately settled on the comfy couch, you remember to peel the curtain back and invite the warm summer sun into the home. After all, what's more asking than the sun giving you a gentle kiss on the cheek before partaking in a fruity espresso with notes of lemon and blackberry?

Now that you've created the perfect haven, you finally gaze up from your nose being buried into the cup and ask your high-school best pal, "So, what happened next?" The conversation between you two is an intimate exchange, both full of shameless tears and gut-wrenching laughter.

Now, open your eyes. Wouldn't that be an ideal Sunday? A day where you have the opportunity to create space for a friendship to blossom and listen to one another talk about the beauty and woes that are inevitably coupled with life. Often it takes dedicated time to cultivate a loving, long-lasting friendship where you can let your curls down and be your authentic self. The foundation of trust and loyalty is laid through years of living life together. These friendships are essential to thrive, and time is needed for relationships to evolve.

But what if I told you that I know someone who wants to be a good friend in Christ to you now? What if I told you that this individual is brave enough to let you in immediately without the years of labor needed to form a genuine friendship? What if I told you that someone you may have never met is willing to share a very personal story with you without knowing if you will be judgmental, but because it sheds a beautiful light on Christ, believes it is worth the sacrifice? What if I told you the person truly exists?

Thankfully, she does exist. She is the author of the book that you have in your hand at this very moment. Ari Gaines is the friend you never knew you had or needed. You will witness the words jump off the pages of her book and resonate in your heart. She has a way of being so relatable that you would think you've known her for years.

I commend my best friend for stepping out on faith and publishing this chapter of her life. The beauty of this book is that it is multifaceted. The narrative will begin to shift depending on where you stand in life. So this is my way of nudging you to read it a few times.

When I first read it years ago, I was hanging on to every word, eager to reach the end to see if this one-sided love story would have a happily ever after. Of course, we are suckers for the perfect ending. But I missed the beauty of the story. I wasn't mature enough to read it through a spiritual lens. I honestly just wanted my best friend to be full of joy, even if that meant experiencing God's promises prematurely.

Then I read this book years later as a young wife in a mature relationship with the Lord. I put on my spiritual glasses the second time and saw that this book is less of a romantic novel and more about how beautifully a relationship between the Father and His daughter is. It illuminates the truth about Lamentations 3:22-23, which says, "The steadfast love of the Lord never ceases; his mercies never come to an end;

they are new every morning, great is your faithfulness."

Ari is a friend that I can count on loving the Lord, and we are so fortunate that she is willing to confirm what we all know to be true: walking alongside the Father isn't always crystal clear and easy, but He is worthy for He gave His only begotten Son to give everlasting life.

Many blessings to you, Ari, a genuine friend and lover of Christ. May God continue to pour His desires into your heart. –

Love,

Nye

To the Reader

This book was the blog that never ended. It holds so many of my life's special moments, and I am honored that you decided to take part in it. This piece is special and unique because it is written primarily in the present. Every word is written through my laughter, tears, joy, and pain. I pray that as you travel with me through time, that you are blessed beyond measure, and most of all, encouraged to cultivate a more intimate relationship with The Father.

Grace and Peace,

The Weight of the Wait

"The journey almost never looks like the destination"

— Ari

The Journey Has Only Begun

Who are you dating?

One night on August 27, 2015, I attended a small group Bible study with my younger cousin, who is more like a brother. This particular night neither of us had much motivation to go but decided to anyway. By the time we arrived, there was no studying going on, just casual conversation. While we were talking, my friend's mom stopped by to pick up her younger brother. She was very reserved the majority of the time, just soaking up our conversation, until suddenly she looked at me and said, "Who are you dating?" Perplexed, I looked behind me to see who she was talking to. Starring right at me she said, "You, I'm talking to you. Who are you dating?" Deeply confused, I respectfully responded and said, no one. She then said, "I see a man, a tall, dark-skinned man. He reminds me of your cousin. He is going to be able to cover you spiritually. I just keep hearing the Lord saying bishop and prophetess."

From this moment, I was utterly blown away. Not only was I not dating anyone, but I had not the slightest idea of who she could have been referring to. I wanted to understand why God would speak to someone about something that may or may not be accurate. Whether this was a false prophecy or not, I had taken hold of it. Something about it resonated in my spirit, yet I had come to a place in my life where my focus was primarily on God. I didn't feel I needed or wanted to even think about a future spouse. I began to drown in my thoughts, trying to figure out who this person could be. Was it my most recent ex? Could it be my crush at the time who was very spiritually mature but was by no means interested in me beyond friendship? It couldn't be; neither one of those people quite fit.

Leaving the house that night, I couldn't wait to talk to my cousin in more depth about everything. As we were riding home, and I began to give him my outlook, he stopped me and said, "Aria... you don't know if it's either one of those people, and guess what, it doesn't even matter, because you try the spirit by the spirit, and God's word will confirm itself." (1 John 4:1)

I agreed, sat back in my seat, and continued to enjoy the night scenery. Then, I quieted my spirit and left it alone. As soon as I did that, I saw flashes of someone. Memories flooded my mind, and, instantly I remembered when I first met this person. I remembered saying he reminded me so much of my cousin, it was scary, and I could never actually date him because of it. It also came to my mind that anytime I would be upset or emotional and praying to God, he would always contact me.

I remembered crying out to God and asking him why I couldn't have a companion on earth. Why couldn't I have a particular person right NOW in my life? I said all that, knowing I wanted to say, GOD, WHERE IS MY HUSBAND!? As if God didn't already know that. As I had my moment, my phone buzzed. It was him, sending me encouraging words. I remembered thinking, wow, God, I guess I have a companion on earth through our friendship. I remembered asking him, what made him text me, and he told me that he just felt it in his spirit. This was always his response when I thought it was God who brought him to me.

At that moment, the flashing memories began to mean something different. Was he the one? After bringing my consciousness back to reality, I remembered the very next day; I was scheduled to take a business trip to Tallahassee. I was dreading taking this four-and-a-half-hour drive, and then it hit me; that's where he was! I remembered texting him about two weeks before to tell him that I would be in town. At that point, things were getting weird. As I was traveling the next day, I somewhat came down from all of my thoughts, well, at least the thoughts of him being the one until the night I saw him.

We planned to meet up at my hotel to catch up a little before he went to the library to study. When he arrived, I came downstairs to meet him. As the elevator doors opened, I couldn't seem to find him. I scaled the room a few times, and then I focused on the left side of the room. With his back turned, sitting in a lobby chair, he looked over his shoulder, and we made eye contact. It was like the entire room stopped, and the feeling I got as we made eye contact encased my whole body. The look on his face was as if he was anxiously awaiting my arrival. In that moment I felt the Holy Spirit say "This is the way he will look at you on your wedding day". Then, as if that wasn't enough for fairy tales, he came over to me, picked me up, and spun me around in excitement. The whole lobby stopped and starred. As he was holding me in his arms, several different thoughts began to flood my mind; I still remember that moment like it was yesterday.

After I regained my composure, we went upstairs. We went through the standard questions anyone would ask when seeing each other for the first time in years, and from there, we began to talk about God. Our conversation seemed as though it would never end. Something was so different about this encounter. Was it what the woman told me? I wasn't sure, but as he talked, the Holy Spirit told me, "Tell him." Immediately I responded in my mind, "Oh no! Hell no! I could never tell him that."

As our conversation went on, I found out that he was dating someone. He was always candid about certain things as they pertained to his life. At that moment, everything I started to believe kind of died. It was fantastic, though, right? But, of course, he didn't know what was said to me in the first place, so it was no big deal. We talked a little more about God, and life, then it was about time for him to leave for the library.

As we walked out to the car to say goodbye, he gave me a hug and a gentle kiss on my forehead. Instantly I felt a strong feeling of adornment. But wait, what am I doing here? He is dating someone. He decided as we were about to part ways that he wanted Chick-Fil-A. Chick-Fil-A is a winner in my book too, so I agreed to go, although I wasn't starving.

During the car ride, we continued to talk about God; our conversation just seemed to flow. It felt like we could talk about anything. I could boldly share my thoughts about God and where I had come, and he did the same. The short trip to the restaurant ended, and he brought me back to the hotel. It was like I didn't want to leave him. I walked back upstairs and prepared for the next day; after all, I was there for work.

As I sat in the room, thoughts of him came rushing into my mind, which I instantly dismissed. I wanted nothing to do with a man who was taking an interest in someone else. No way could God be showing me a man who belonged to another woman. Before I could even live in that space, I remembered thinking, girl, stop; he could be still showing me him. Maybe that was the Holy Spirit. Shortly after I shut my brain off, I felt the spirit again, quietly saying, "You have to tell him." That's how you know when it's the Father. His voice is so quiet and subtle (1 Kings 19:11-13). I was stubborn, of course, so I shut that down once again and continued with my nightly routine. I did a little reading and started to focus my energy back to where it was before, or at least try to.

The next day during my training, we were texting, and I told him I wanted to hang out. He asked me what I wanted to do. I don't recall my response, but I'm sure I had a nice list of things. He then asked me if I wanted to hang out at the house. Instantly being the passive-aggressive person that I am, I asked him was he trying to hide me? He responded and said, of course not! There will be a lot of people there, even my girlfriend. Instantly something came over me, and I asked myself again, what is going on here, what am I doing? I am by no means a person that wants to disrespect anyone's relationship. I knew I felt different about him with this most recent encounter. No way could I be around his significant other, so I declined the invite.

The next day I continued to think of him, so I texted. He told me he wanted to see me and how there was a fashion show that he wanted me to go to. Very early on in our friendship, modeling was something we talked about a lot. He knew it was always a dream of mine to have a thriving modeling career. His girlfriend would be at this event as well, so of course, I declined. Not because of anything shady, but more so out of respect for her space. I never intended to take an interest in him the way I did. Then he told me we could go out later that evening. He and I would hit the town with a few of his friends, so I decided to go.

He picked me up, and we headed to the house to meet a few of his friends. I knew there would be people close to his girlfriend, so I made sure to mingle with everyone to avoid any confusion or misunderstandings. They were fun people, but even with my efforts to try and be respectful, there was still something that continued to draw us together. Even in a large crowd, I could feel him close, and we had never even shared an intimate hug. Of these moments as we were out, there was a time that I was sitting with him, and again I heard "Tell him." As we conversed, I said to him, you know it's something I want to tell you, but I don't know if I should. He then proceeded to tell me a story of how his father told him whenever you have something to say, you should say it because you may never get the opportunity again. I told him that was cute, but I still didn't want to tell him.

We left the first location, which was a social bar, and went to a place with more of a club feel.

By this time, I had already been asked a million questions by his girlfriend's friend, but for some reason, it never made me feel uncomfortable. I never once felt a tense moment. We had a great time at the party; he sat the entire time and didn't dance much. I could tell he was in deep thought the entire night.

We left the party and then got a bite to eat with a few of his friends at Guthrie's, where the chicken fingers were glorious, if I must say so. After getting food, we dropped his friends off and went back to his place to eat. As we sat in his room, the conversation flowed as usual. I probably talked trash about Ole Miss beating Bama just the year before. Speaking of Bama, let's take a journey back to undergrad when we first met. Do you remember in the introduction where I mentioned how he told me something that would later change my life forever?

Kephir
Young Lioness

While completing my undergraduate degree, I was also a member of the track team at Ole Miss. God blessed me to have such a fantastic opportunity. The way I ended up, there was nothing short of a blessing. The word tells us that our gifts will make room for us (Psalm 18:16), and in this situation, my gift led me to my future husband, amongst many other things.

We were at Drake relays in April of 2011. My very close friend and teammate met someone from another team, and he wanted to hang out once she made it back to the hotel. The hotel looked like some type of track and field convention. Anytime you would leave the room, there were teams everywhere. She didn't want to meet up with her friend alone, so after some convincing, I went.

Before I get into this story, let me give you a little glimpse into the collegiate track world. In my opinion, track and field is one of the most social collegiate sports. I say this because it's one of the few where both the men's and women's teams travel together. The track meets often last up to four days, and athletes most likely will not compete each day of the meet. While traveling, you have a little time on your hands if you are done with shakeouts, practice, or competition. Most teams would mingle with other schools during their downtime; it just became the nature of the travel atmosphere.

Okay, back to the story. We met up with her friend, and things flowed the way most initial encounters would. My roommate's friend had a roommate as well, so the meeting wasn't as awkward. We introduced ourselves and talked a little about the events we competed in. As we sat there talking, my best friend's roommate began to tell my friend what her personality was like; the topic kind of came out of nowhere. I remembered asking him, "So if you know all that about her, then tell me about my personality too." That was when he would speak the words that would define something about me that was so much deeper than I thought. I will never forget how he broke everything down. He said," You, you're like a lioness; you walk gracefully and calmly. You watch a lot of the things around you, but when somebody messes with you, you strike! I remember him making a whole claw motion and roaring, but I digress.

I'm sure by now you're thinking, that's it!? That's the moment that defined the essence of your existence? You can see how I wouldn't think much of what was said either, but one thing I did know was that he discerned everything that was spoken; he didn't know me. After our initial encounter, he and I kept in touch through social media and occasional texts. We saw each other at a few track meets, and I traveled to see him once. He was always so positive. He always kept me in check when I would get down on myself about the way I competed. He would always say, give thanks, to God be the glory I always admired his faith but never saw the gem he was back then.

That summer after we met, I went to visit him at school. I guess the trip wasn't really about him and I because I was a tag-along, but it still was a fun trip. The trip felt somewhat awkward at times, because I liked him very much, but just as my friend. At the time, I was so wrapped up in exploring things with my boyfriend in college, who was not my boyfriend at the time, but I was emotionally attached to him. Nevertheless, we had a wonderful time. We went to the movies to see Columbiana and walked around the campus. One of the evenings, we went to watch him and a few of his teammates play pickup soccer. It was a beautiful evening; I remembered sitting on the bleachers with my best friend meditating on life. This trip was the first time I thought; I could never date him; he reminds me too much of my younger cousin.

That weekend ended, and we continued to keep in touch, but I never visited again. He always seemed to have been dating someone after that, and the same for me. Time went on, and we didn't communicate as much, but he was always there whenever I needed him. I remember intentionally finding scripture that represented the way I felt about our friendship, Proverbs 27:9. I sent him a bracelet with the scripture on it and a little saying that he would always tell me, "A-team." I never actually knew why he would say it so often.

I remember my first indoor meet of my senior season. I had been working hard during the off-season. I was physically and mentally prepared to put out some excellent marks that year. The week of the track meet came around, and not only did I unknowingly tear a muscle in my quad, but I left my triple jump spikes at my apartment in Oxford. All of my spike bags looked the same besides my scribbles on the Nike check denoting each of my events; sadly, I grabbed my sprint spikes. For everyone familiar with track and field, I'm sure you cringed at the thought of me triple jumping in sprint spikes. It would have probably been better for me not to jump at all. I began to panic, and I'm not sure why, but I thought of him as I brainstormed a plan. I texted and told him what happened, he replied and said he would see what he could do. He was able to get spikes from one of his teammates, who I was competing against! Now that I have given you some background, and went a little off track, let's get back to the story.

We laughed and enjoyed the evening as we sat in his room, but it was getting late. As I sat there, I remembered telling him earlier that evening that there was something I wanted to share. I never said anything about it, but he didn't forget and reminded me of it. Despite my determination to keep this from him, there was something still tugging at me just to say it. I have never known of revelations like this, so I felt weird sharing. That didn't stop his curiosity. He kept asking and bet me that if he could throw his shirt over to his hamper, I would have to tell him. The hamper was across the room in the closet under hanging clothes. I thought to myself, "There is no way this dude is going to make this shot; I'm good." It never crossed my mind that maybe he takes that shot all the time. I was setting myself up for failure, and of course, he made it.

I took a deep breath and thought of explaining what was said to me without sounding like a desperate weirdo. Instead, I told him everything the best way I knew how. I told him how he didn't even come to mind when everything was being said. The visions I saw of him in the car did not come from me; it had to be God. He stopped me as I was explaining and said, "Aria," with his prominent Jamaican accent, "Are you saying I'm your knight in shining armor?" I told him that I didn't know. That was all so odd to me. He said the same thing my cousin said about trying the spirit by the spirit and that God confirms his word. At that moment, I didn't even care if he was my husband or not; I was just relieved to have gotten everything off my chest.

We talked a little more about life. He started talking about a specific prophetic word he received about his life that he never really got into the details about. During that conversation, he began to talk about what he knew he needed from his future wife. He said, "I need a strong woman, Aria are you strong?" How does someone even answer that even if you are strong? I replied yes, and he went on to explain why he felt he needed that. He definitely can be intimidating if you don't understand spiritual things. Whenever he explains something, he asks a question first. Then, he would say, "What does the Bible say about this...."? Usually, I knew exactly what the answer was, but I would hesitate because he asked like a scrutinizing professor many times. He is a strong person, and it's not a coincidence that he realizes that quality will be necessary for his wife. As we continued to talk, it was getting later and later. Finally, I told him I had to go and began to gather my things to leave. I remember him saying, "No! I'm not ready for you to go". I didn't want to leave either, but I wanted to be respectful of his relationship.

As we got back in the car, we continued to converse. He said something about A-Team, the name he would always call me when we were in undergrad. I asked him what made him always say A-team. He explained to me that there were many things he could say when addressing me, a lot of nicknames that could easily be for someone else. He told me it was so that I would always

16

know that it was for me. At that moment, I couldn't help but smile. As we were riding in the car headed to the hotel, he said to me, "I didn't take you to see the facilities!" so we turned around and drove to campus. He showed me the football stadium, which was pretty impressive, and a few other places, and then we pulled up to the track stadium.

Let Jah Moon Come Shining

As we got closer, He told me the gate is usually locked, but we would check anyway. When we pulled up, the gate was cracked open. We walked in, and I couldn't help but notice how beautiful it was. Whenever I am in an open space, I become the biggest kid you can imagine. I want to flip and run in the grass barefoot. I was so wild as a kid; my mom always fussed at me about running around with no shoes on. I guess there was a piece of that still in me. As we walked in, I looked at him and said, "I bet you won't race me." He looked at me like, are you kidding? "Let's Go!" I still had my heels on, so I told him he had to take his shoes off too. We walked down the track about 50 meters and stopped. He gave me about a 5-meter head start and let me call us off.

On your mark, set, go! And we were off; I think he underestimated my speed. He started laughing so hard that it took him a little more effort than he thought to beat me. We both were laughing uncontrollably as he yelled, "why do I have to turn on my speed to beat you?" He did win but, not by a whole lot. The distance between us is still up for debate. It was the most careless fun I had in a long time. It was so liberating; the moment reminded me of playing outside in the street as a kid. After racing, he looked at me and said, "You did the long jump in college, right?" I paused before I said yes; I knew he was thinking of something crazy, and of course, he asked to have a jump-off. I refused, but something in me wanted to just go near the pit. I missed track so much. This was my first time back on a collegiate track since college.

The grass was wet, and I was thinking of every excuse not to walk over to the pit, so he carried me on his back, and we went over. He told me I could jump from wherever I wanted. I did a short run-up and jumped. I felt like I was flying. I could feel how high I was; the jump felt effortless. He jumped after me and beat me by a couple of feet. He wanted to go again, and I said I was done. He kept saying one more time! And If I win you have to give me something. I asked what, and he wouldn't tell me. He told me that I just had to trust him, I agreed. I remember thinking if it were something outlandish, I would just refuse.

19

Long story short, I jumped again. That moment in the air felt amazing. I remember him yelling, "Whoa, you jumped so far!"

I jumped farther than his mark from before. At this point, he was pumped. He started doing warm-up drills and telling me that there was no way he would let me beat him. This competitive turn was so funny to watch. He jumped again and beat me by about 8 inches. He celebrated for a bit, and then we walked back to the place where our stuff was. As we were walking, he squatted down and told me to get on his shoulders. I looked at him like he was crazy. He continued to urge me, so I did. It was so scary; I hadn't been on someone's shoulders since I was a kid; my dad used to do it all the time. He reached for my hands and began to spin around in circles. All I could do was scream; it was so liberating. He put me down, and we began to walk around the track. He reached for my hand, and we walked and talked. I told him how much I missed track and felt something was missing as if I needed to go back. At the time, he was training professionally and preparing for the 2016 Summer Olympics. In this moment of walking and talking with him, things just felt right.

I remember wondering how we could see with barely any lights, and then I saw the moon.

It was complete and hovering right over us. The sight was breathtaking. Since then, I have never looked at a full moon the same. Anytime I get discouraged about this journey, and start to lose hope, I see it, and I'm reminded of God's promise. *On the most improbable night, God was there to bring us light.* I recollect sitting with him on a plyo box and him saying to me, "I'm going back and forth with myself about whether I should get what I want" I asked him why, and he said he didn't know. I knew somewhat what he was referring to because we started talking about relationships. He told me he knew I would leave and find someone else.

He went on to tell me how he has never liked anyone as quickly as me. He said, I know you, but I don't know you. We have known each other for a while, but I have never spent any time with you to see who you are. I agreed but felt this weird feeling in my soul of uncertainty. That feeling brought me back to reality, and I made up my mind not to live in the fairytale place I have always allowed myself to abide in. At this point, it was almost 4:00 am, and we needed to leave before we got in trouble for being there. He took me back to the hotel, and we said our goodbyes. He kept saying he wanted me to stay and go to church, but I felt it was best to head back home the following day.

That Sunday, on my drive home, I remember playing my worship music. I began to pray in the spirit about everything that occurred over the weekend. I was brought to uncontrollable tears; I didn't know why I was crying or what was happening. I felt so sure about where I was in Christ, and now I was questioning everything. Soon after I made it back home, I began to receive confirmation about what God was trying to show me.

Ari Gideon Gaines

1 John 4:1-5

Dear friends, do not believe every spirit but test the spirits to see whether they are from God because many false prophets have gone out into the world.

There is a story in the Bible that you may have heard people talk about. It describes Gideon and how he was having trouble believing word from the Lord. During this part of my journey, I felt like Gideon's long-lost twin sister. When reading Judges 6:33-40, it's difficult not to think to yourself, is this guy serious? Of course, God is giving him exactly what he is asking for, and he still doesn't believe it, but I found myself there.

One of the first confirmations I received was when I got back from the trip. I remember taking a trip to the Atlanta Zoo on Labor Day with my childhood best friend and son. The day was perfect. We went to dinner after the zoo and talked about everything that went on during my trip. I shared how my soul felt free with him, how everything felt surreal, but at the same time, our reality was very different from what I felt. Her responses in this conversation were very sound. They left me feeling confident about my place in what seemed to be chaos. I have always appreciated her undying love for me regardless of how often we spend time. Our conversation calmed me from all of the anxiety and encouraged me to continue pushing.

The next day my grandmother yelled out to me from the kitchen that I had a package. That moment when you know you didn't buy anything but your online shopping habits have been so outrageous in the past, you never know. I really didn't purchase anything though. I went to her to take the package and opened it. To my utter surprise he sent me a Bible. After all of my questioning and spending an entire day thinking of him, I received a Bible. I was shocked. The Bible was my favorite color, and it had my name engraved on the front.

When I texted him to thank him, he said to me, "I'm not sure if you write in your Bible, but I want you to mark this one up, and highlight. I hope that God will show you wonders as you read, and grow old with this Bible". His words were so heartfelt. So I began to read that Bible, and not because he told me to. This version of the Bible seemed so easy to retain. As I began to read more, my understanding grew immensely, and in return, my relationship with God soared to higher heights.

Finally, as we were texting, I asked him what made him send it, and he gave that same line I always got; the spirit told him to do it. As I continued to pour myself into my Bible, I recalled someone from my small group telling me that I had the spirit of Esther. As I was doing my daily reading, I decided to read about her in more detail. I knew a little about the story but not specifics. As I was reading, I came across Esther 1:19.

Also, let the King give her royal position to someone else who is better than her.

This is what my heart was harboring. I couldn't grasp that a good God would show me my husband was someone who had no interest in being more than my friend. He was showing me someone who was in a relationship. The Queen was summoned to dinner, and she didn't show because it was degrading for a Middle Eastern woman to be present when there was wine flowing freely at celebrations for the King. She was to be secluded during times like this one. Vashti not coming to the party enraged the King and caused her to be removed. God used this unfortunate outcome for Vashti, for the good of his people. The incident that led to her removal was just the catalyst of something that was already destined. This was when God revealed to me that relationships that he chooses are called to a high purpose. He showed me that I didn't have to worry about it regardless of what it looked like.

"You are the Queen", He said to me. This revelation came during my edits (12.18.17). The original day I received this confirmation was September 9, 2015, one day after receiving the Bible in the mail. In that moment, I still managed to convince myself that it was the devil using scripture to make me hold on to the things I wanted in my heart, so I let it go. Looking back at this, it's crazy how we will allow the enemy to sneak in and snatch away the truth God has given us. That night if I had stopped doubting, would this journey be different?

Time went on, and I continued to read different books to continue to strengthen my spiritual growth. One particular night I was reading the book of Joshua. As I was reading, I heard The Spirit say to me, "Send him the book." I knew the book He was referring to. It was called *I Kissed Dating Goodbye*. Instantly I said, No! I'm not going to send him a book that would make it seem like I wanted him to leave the person he is with. I remembered saying, Lord, if you want me to send him this book, you will have to come down from heaven and show me. Then The Spirit said, "look at the author of the book." I froze; no way is the name of this author Joshua. I hopped out of bed and scrambled through my backpack where I kept the book, and there it was, Joshua Harris. In total shock, I knew I had to be *obedient*.

I ordered the book on September 24 and sent it to him. I wrote the bookstore where I ordered the book, asking them to please place a note inside. I did that so I could someway not make myself look crazy. After putting in the order, I waited. Time went by, and I hadn't heard from him. Finally, he sent me a random text asking if I found a 100 dollar bill, what I would do with it. He is constantly probing people. During that text conversation, I asked him when was the last time he checked his mail. He texted back and said, "it was you! It was you who sent the book!" Not only was my note not in the book, but my name wasn't on the return to sender address either. He said he thought the book was sent from God; I guess maybe it was. He said I should have never told him that I was the one who sent it because he thought it was a sign from God. I told him the Lord put it on my heart to send it, and he responded with something dry. I could tell when he didn't receive certain things.

This moment was the last I would hear from him for a little while until my birthday that year. He called briefly to say happy birthday, and that was about it. After that, we talked a little more on and off. I called him a few times during 2016 about some things I was dealing with. But by that time, I had somewhat given up on what God was showing me. He was still dating the same person, and I felt in my spirit that he would never receive what God was showing me. I kept thinking about humans and how we have free will to choose what we want. He had chosen differently, and that would be the result of this fate. The hurt of letting go was much easier than keeping the faith and carrying that burden, so I chose to walk away.

GPS Detour

In around March of 2016, I began to feel very discontent with my job at the time. I felt like there was no growth, so I began to look for work elsewhere. In this search, I was in no hurry to leave if the situation wasn't just right, but I soon found out that my desire to go was not just because of me. There was a bigger purpose behind it. Some things occurred that only God could have orchestrated.

One day I walked into work, and my supervisor pretty much told me on a Monday that I may not get paid that Wednesday. Long story short, during this time of trying to figure out why my check was being put in jeopardy when I worked the hours, I was told that this was the nature of the job. The situation became very uncomfortable, and I was forced to look for something else. After leaving, I was granted a full-time internship opportunity at the University of Miami in the field I was looking to go back into. During the interview process, I removed my application from the candidate pool due to financial circumstances.

Around that same time, my brother visited Miami and was training with the baseball team at his Alma Mater. For some reason, he loved wearing this trucker cap that had the logo from my job at the time on the front. One day at practice, one of the coaches asked him what it was. He told him it was where I worked, but that I was thinking about getting back into academic support. His friend went on to say to him that he knew someone that worked at Miami, and he would get in touch with her for me. My brother was aware that I had retracted my application. He told me at that moment; he knew I had to call back. He called me that same day and told me to call the school back. I explained to him all the reasons why I couldn't for how embarrassing it would be. He replied most funnily and said, "What do you have to lose? You don't have a job anymore?" My brother is always so blatant when I'm lost in my thoughts. That's exactly what I need from him in moments like this one. He was right; I knew what I had to do. I contacted the search committee director and asked to be placed back into the candidate pool. I went through each step of the hiring process and got the job.

I knew there was something more to this position. I knew God had something special planned for me, but I didn't quite know what. While being in Miami, I was living with my brother's fiancé and her family who always felt like my own. They were gracious in allowing me to live with them. My time in Miami was exciting. As soon as I got there, I started visiting a church and attempted to stay on the path, but that slowly changed.

I started to drift away from my relationship with God. I stopped going to church and started going out more, probably more than I ever have. There was something about Miami that appealed to my flesh. The nightlife there was so inviting in the way that it was such a calm atmosphere. The music was diverse, and so were the people. It was beautiful; I felt, why not? I'm not doing anything wrong. This brings me back to something I have heard a pastor say; it is not about whether or not you can; it's about whether or not you should (1 Corinthians 10:23). It started as me just going out and enjoying friends to compromising my sexual purity. It's all fun and games until someone gets hurt.

One night I was out with my best friend, who I met in high school. She is from Miami and just so happened to move back around the same time I moved there. We were enjoying a girl's night out, not really dancing or anything, just enjoying the atmosphere when a guy approached, who unbeknownst to me was my fruit from the forbidden tree, and man did I bite. This is a perfect example of how something can seem innocent, and it just grows into something bigger more detrimental (James 1:15).

Then, after desire has conceived, it gives birth to sin; and sin, when it is full-grown, gives birth to death.

The enemy doesn't just throw things in your face; he is crafty. He knew spiritually I wasn't in a place where I was taking crap from anyone, but emotionally I was lonely. I hadn't gotten the fullness of what it meant to be in love with God. There was a crack in my foundation. He used that crack to sneak in and drain me of what felt like everything I gained since that moment on June 28, 2015, when I decided to fall deeply in love with God. This particular love interest was nothing short of intriguing, charming, and funny. He was different from a lot of the men I had encountered before. His lighthearted personality opened a door I would have never thought would have given access to my detour. The devil may not be able to change God's destiny for our lives, but he definitely can prolong it by keeping us distracted through the poor decisions we make.

I began to allow the feeling of loneliness that was tucked away in my heart to grow. An excellent book called Purpose Awakening by Touré Roberts speaks about different perspectives for different people and how you never know what you are capable of until you have been placed in certain situations. In this time, God showed me that something in me allowed me to walk away from his teachings and go down a different path. If I was never placed in the environment I was in, I would have never known that those things were inside me. They would likely have just laid dormant, only to come out at the most inopportune time.

Don't get what I am saying confused; God won't put you in a position to sin. The Bible says that God will never tempt us (James 1:13). God may be trying to show us things about who we are, and it's up to us to see it. The word tells us that God will always offer a way out. He provided me plenty of back doors, front doors, windows, fire escapes, you name it, but I decided to ignore it. I should have removed myself from the situation in those red flag moments, but since I wasn't truly content with my place in God, I allowed other things to infiltrate my life. I didn't stay the course, and I paid for it. God is so merciful and always forgiving. Anytime I have fallen, he has picked me back up and embraced me all the more, but the walk back to that place is what was challenging.

There are both negative and positive consequences to our actions (Galatians 6:7). The result I had to deal with was the soul tie I created with a person that was never meant to be my husband. Breaking the bonds that I made in this relationship was very difficult, and it took quite some time for me to get over it. I felt very depressed and displaced, but my father wouldn't let me stay there. God's mercies are new each day (Lamentations 3:22-23). As I continued to heel and move forward, I would speak to a good friend of mine, who I met through my other best friend from high school. My time in Miami was coming to an end, and the Friday right before I headed home, we planned to meet up for dinner. By this time, I had let go of any hope of who I thought was "The One". I was convinced that there was for sure someone else out there for me, even if my current situation didn't work out, until that night at dinner.

We sat down at the bar and began talking and laughing as usual. He asked me had I been blogging, and I told him that I had. Just the night before, I started a blog that didn't seem to end. He wanted to know more, but I was apprehensive; nevertheless, I did. I soon remembered what urged me to write the book. On Tuesday, June 27, 2017, I left connect group, thinking about my old friend, so I gave him a call. We had somewhat lost touch; he made me feel too vulnerable. It just felt all wrong to reach out to him consistently, but this night I called. We talked on the phone for over 2 hours. The conversation was emancipating.

God revealed something to him about Adam and Eve from Genesis 2:21-23. He spoke about how Adam came to after his deep sleep. Eve had been presented to him, and he trusted God enough to see that she was his wife. Furthermore, he trusted that God made her with all of the qualities that were desirable to him. He was even blown away by how profound the revelation was. During this conversation, the beauty of marriage was restored in my heart. I stopped believing marriage was special before this moment, and frankly, I stopped caring about the day I would get married. This revelation was just so astounding it made my heart smile. I felt like God was showing me not to see marriage differently than the way He intended it to be.

I began to give the background story about my friend and the word I felt I received from the Lord. He was eating and not paying attention until I told him everything from the night of the prophecy. He stopped me as I was finishing the story and told me to start over. I noticed he wasn't focused, and he later said to me that the spirit said to him, "Listen to her, pay attention." As I began to tell the story again, he looked at me with this shocked face and said, "So what you're saying is you're already spoken for?" I asked him what he meant, and he said, "So basically, this dude is your husband." Hearing someone else say it made me feel weird, very weird. Then he told me that the problem was that I already knew, and because of my lack of faith, I was the hold-up. At this point, he had my attention. My thoughts of walking away from the word the Lord had given me almost two years ago were dissipating with every word he spoke. He looked at me and said that I was special, and there was a reason why God revealed the union to me first. He said, "You are like a lion, like a lioness." Instantly all I could think about was when my friend told me I was like a lioness the first day I met him. I shared that, and he responded saying, "Do you think it's a coincidence that he was the first person to tell you that?"

The encouragement I received not to doubt the situation made me feel so confident in what I felt in my heart to be valid from before. It was like I buried it into the deepest parts of my heart, but it wasn't dead; it was just buried alive. As we were ending our conversation, he told me when we met; the Lord said to him, "Leave this one alone, she is not for you, but there are some things I need you to do for her." After hearing that, I didn't care anything about knowing who my husband was and whether or not I was a psycho for believing it. I could only think of how much God must love me. Him wanting to make it known that I was to be protected made me feel nothing less than special and adorned.

I left Miami that Sunday evening feeling empty and somewhat lost about my current situation. I settled in, but my time home was brief because my cousins wedding was the following weekend. As my family drove to New Orleans, I thought deeply, reading my book and meditating. Little did I know God took a personal seat right next to me during the ride. I was reading a chapter In *Purpose Awakening* that spoke about the ways to discover your purpose. It talked about God knowing exactly what he created you for and how he has named every one of his creations. I remembered in 2015, right before the prophecy was given to be I began to sign my journal as Ari. I started a blog at the beginning of January 2016 that used the name as well. I even looked up the meaning, but I never thought twice about it. Something in my soul made me feel that God was showing me my name, but I never looked deeper. As I continued to read, I felt the spirit drop me a nugget, as my Aunt would say, and my whole world shifted. The book speaks about the journey in your purpose and how the Lord will change your name. I remembered thinking, oh like how I began to use Ari? Then it hit me like a ton of bricks. Ari means lion of God! God sees me—Aria, as a lioness. Then I heard the spirit say, *"This was who you were to me before it was ever revealed to either of your friends. This is how I have always seen you; It is who I created you to be."*

That word changed my life forever. Unspeakable joy is what I felt in my heart. I felt a special love and adornment from God. Words don't express the feeling in my soul that day; I felt like his baby girl. I was so astonished tears began to roll down my face. God is such an awesome God, and if we would just be in place for him to reach us, we can reach unfathomable heights. It's almost like having a walkie-talkie; you have to be in range to hear what is being said. God wants us to know how very much he loves us, but sometimes we step out of range. I encourage you to make a declaration today to get closer. Tune into God's station, and be prepared to receive his passionate love messages to you.

While visiting New Orleans, I was able to have some alone time with my brother and tell him all the things that were revealed to me. He had total excitement on his face and support in his voice. Telling this story to someone who I love so dearly was essential to me. Julius seeing the spiritual side of everything made the thoughts I had about feeling crazy not so embarrassing. My brother has a very calm spirit. He doesn't always say much, but I know he is watching. After leaving New Orleans and returning to Georgia, I knew I had to start my life again. I knew I had to dig deep and move forward. Then a series of events occurred that kept me in place of defeat. In turn I began to doubt again.

Never in my life have I felt so profoundly saddened than the time it took me to get over the guy I met while living in Miami. There is something that happens in the soul of a woman when she has attached herself to someone emotionally and physically. We create in our minds what our lives will be like with that person. We plan everything without ever clarifying anything with God or the person we see inevitably creating false realities. I was in a very dark place, trying to move on from what I thought I had with this person. I would think of him constantly, but I knew I couldn't stay in this place. I began to pick myself up and do what I knew to heal my heart. I gave it back to The One who created it. I would spend more time with my family and friends, but most importantly with God. I began to allow myself to get excited about work and pouring my purpose into everything I did. Life became beautiful again. This situation made me understand the principle of why God wants us to stay on a particular path. It's not just wrapped in purpose; God doesn't want to see us hurting and struggling, but guess who does? Straying from the path won't cause me to go to hell, but I went through hell trying to get through it.

Weight
of
Wait

As I began to move on and live my life in the present, I kept hearing and reading about how God doesn't choose your spouse for you, which is valid to a certain extent. God will not choose for you; He never does it is always our choice; however, we have to remember that God knows the end at the beginning, and he has no issue showing us who we will CHOOSE to marry.

Isaiah 46:10

I make known the end from the beginning, from ancient times, what is still to come. I say, 'My purpose will stand, and I will do all that I please.'

We as humans take our little tiny brains and devise that God showing us our spouse is giving you a choice, and it's not. He is showing you who you WILL choose, just like with Adam. God didn't make Eve, Ana, and Stacey and then tell Adam to choose; he made one woman. He made Eve with all of the qualities Adam needed and desired, and then he presented her to him (Genesis 2:22).

I continued to hear that God wouldn't show you who your spouse was, and I started to let

41

doubt creep in even more. We always have to remember that once we have identified the voice of the Lord, we must stand firm in the belief of what he has shown us. God knew the place I was in, and he reminded me of a book that I read right before reading "I Kissed Dating Goodbye." The book was called "Preparing to Be a Help Meet." When I ordered the book, I remembered all the reviews saying the book was great for single, dating, and married women. At that time, I heard so much about preparing for a marriage that I felt compelled to read it. Little did I know as I began to read the book, the author talks about how the Lord showed her who her husband was at the age of 12! She attended a youth conference where he preached when the Lord said that he would be her husband. The book talks about how she went home and told her mother. Her mom said that if he were to be her husband, she would need to remember to pray for him, and she posted the church flyer on the refrigerator.

She went on to work closely with him, as he had become the lead pastor in her church. She many times had to watch him date other women. He never even really showed interest in her. Even though her situation had many moments of disappointments and frustrations, she still held to what she believed in her heart, and eventually, they got married. It was like God was trying to show me in my moment of doubt that He does tell us who our future spouses will be, and his word does manifest. I ordered this book before I even knew anything about my future husband.

GPS Reroute

This situation takes faith. We are NEVER in consistent communication. With all things considered, I have gotten to a point where I no longer care to linger over whether the word God gave me about my husband is true or if God will answer my final prayer for confirmation. I feel as though the most important thing to me is exploring and deepening my intimate relationship with God. Strengthening myself as a woman of God for whoever my husband is. If I know anything from the things I have shared in this book, God will bring His promise to me in whatever mysterious way he pleases.

I never intended to cross paths with my friend the times I did. God could have done that; who knows. Who is to say that He isn't capable of bringing us both together in due time, but I don't want to live my life harboring thoughts of him and trying to finagle my way into his heart. What God speaks to me is for me. God is not a liar; what He says will come forth with time. Never in the Bible does it say to dwell on something until it comes to fruition. I believe that God can bring people you are meant to marry into your life, but I can't say that I am 100% sure that I will marry this person. I do feel God is able; I don't know for sure if it's him. I think God will show me what he needs to show me, and there will be nothing that can stand in the way of that. Until that time, I will remain in him and allow him to do what needs to be done.

It is my job to stay focused. I want to become the woman God would have for me to be before I am the woman someone else needs me to be. I want to indulge myself in the things of the Lord completely. I want to feel and understand his love for me. That's what I want, and with time the Lord will bring my husband. Until then the words on these pages can be words that are completely insane, or they will be words from the Lord meant for a testimony for anyone out there waiting for God to manifest things in their lives. So I guess we will have to wait and see 9.12.17.

Just Wait?

The words I ended the last chapter with are exciting, shaping the entirety of this chapter. For a very long time, my mindset has been that we should wait on the Lord, and he will renew our strength. Just believe, and you will receive. I thought these things, not truly knowing what it meant to have faith and believe. Many of us have heard the scripture; without faith, it is impossible to please God. For as long as I have listened to scriptures, Hebrews 4 has resonated with me. Out of all the famous verses, we learn this one clearly states what is pleasing to God. I have always wanted my life to be good to God regardless of if it was or not. Despite my efforts, I always felt I wasn't doing this faith thing right. I felt like something must have been wrong or missing. My understanding of faith was to believe and not have doubt. For a long time, I would go back and forth about whether I truly believed something. When I felt like I thought whole-heartedly, without a doubt, it had to mean I had faith, right? Wrong, the word says faith without works is dead James 2:17. Having faith that God showed me who my husband was and then just sitting on it isn't exactly what God wanted me to do. It is when you move on your faith that things change. Look at it this way; God may tell you one day that you will own a business. You can have all the faith in the world, but nothing will happen if you don't make a business plan. It's like the man who buried his talents (Matthew 25:14-30). Don't bury the things the Lord has given you because you didn't walk in faith.

One day on 9.29.17, I needed to stop by my brother's job to pick something up. A close family friend of ours was there, so I sat and chatted with him a bit. He asked me was I happy with my job. I told him that I was, but my ultimate goal was my future business. From there, we started a conversation that would take me on a journey that I would have never expected. He began to tell me a story about a favorite restaurant of his where there are paintings of black men all over the walls. He noticed how the countenance of these men seemed to be depressed and troubled. He asked the Lord why they seemed so down, and the Lord replied that it was because they all had dreams and purpose that were unfulfilled.

He then began to tell me about when he first started his business. There were a few things that weren't necessarily going as planned. He began to pray about everything, and the Lord told him to get off of his knees and take action. He would always have a good story when taking me through the things God has revealed to him. He then brought everything back to my business, and said what are you doing with your business? I told him all we had prepared, but then I realized that I wasn't doing much of anything. He told me that my faith meant doing, even if it was only a little at a time.

Earlier that week, my brother told me the same thing in relation to reaching out to my "old friend". I told him we had spoken over the summer right before I moved home from Miami. During that phone call, he mentioned me coming to visit. We never spoke again after that day, but I remembered him asking me if it was bad that he needed to set a reminder to text me about when would be a good time to visit. Julius replied in his calm "duh voice," "Well, did you remind him?" I paused and realized that I never did. I knew from these two conversations that I needed to reach out to him, so I did. When I finally mustered up the courage, I didn't have any time for small talk. I felt like that would give room to talk myself out of asking. When he responded, it was as if he really could care less if I came or not. To protect myself I left it alone. I figured if God wanted us to come together, He would indeed show that to him too. During this period, I continued to focus on myself and moved on with life, or so I thought.

_____ *Miles to Destination*

11.25.17

I would never have thought the Lord showing me how he viewed me would cause so many revelations in such a short period. I still don't think I understand the depths of what it means to be a lion of God, but because that is what my father sees me as I began to study lions. I found that a pack of lions is called a pride; I began to see the traits of a lioness and her role in the pride. The lioness is the breadwinner of the pack. She is called to do things that one with a carnal mind about the "order" of duties in a family would find unorthodox. Seeing this helped me realize that I will still be called to my husband in the way God would have for me too, but that my role would be very significant to our family.

The Lord has brought many special people into my life during this new phase of my journey, a couple of them being the family friend who spoke to me about faith that night at my brother's facility and his family. They are pretty much like an aunt and uncle. From my initial conversation with Uncle B about the faces on the wall in the restaurant, I never would have thought that he would be such a vital part of this journey. In this challenging time, it seemed like only they knew how to support me in certain moments. Long story short, because I know you guys are wondering where I am going with this, there are two very huge lessons that the Lord has shown me in just two months. This all has happened since I last edited this journeyed memoir.

One day on my usual route home, I went to see my brother at work. Uncle B was there, but that day he was occupied by another conversation. After about an hour, I figured it was about time for me to go home, so I went to say my goodbyes and, he looked at me with that look your parents give you as a teen when you are trying to walk out of the house too late, and he said, "Where are you going?" I told him home, but he managed to change my mind. From that moment, we were chatting and ended up planning a short notice family dinner.

As we made dinner arrangements, he asked me, "What is the father telling you about dating"? Anytime he asks me a question, there is ALWAYS a deeper meaning behind it, so I knew where this conversation was headed. I felt confident that it was time to tell him everything I felt the Lord showing me. I told him it was a long story, and I wanted to tell him and Aunt Lo together. He insisted that he would tell her the story. I knew after hearing the long story; there was no way he would still feel that way after.

Nevertheless, I summed it up the best way I knew how. We planned to meet everyone for dinner at his family's favorite Jamaican restaurant. I thought that was kind of ironic and a little funny. As I began to tell him everything, he became reticent. We reached the restaurant, and the only thing he said to me was that I needed to get my pride out of the way. This wouldn't be the first time I heard that, so I received what he said. Once we got to the restaurant, he encouraged me to tell Aunt Lo the story. As I told her everything, she seemed to be very captivated, and at the very end, she said to me, "Wow! Now that's a story; you have to finish that book."

A Lioness's Pride

      That same dinner weekend, I spent the day with Uncle B and Julius at a baseball showcase. At the showcase, we began to talk about my life journey. We would talk a little, and then we would leave the conversation alone. It was like he couldn't figure out why my friend and I weren't in a relationship. As the day went on, we ended with a late lunch. I could tell Uncle B was very puzzled by my current situation, and he said to me. "I feel like you've told him about 60%, but you never told him about the confirmations God gave you, did you?" At that moment, there were so many things swirling around in my mind. How could I have overlooked the fact that the Lord gave me all of those confirmations for a reason? I always felt the Lord was showing me everything because he was expecting something from me, but I never had the urge to act. I couldn't help but think about how I had to tell him everything after being swerved about a month before. At that moment the pride, and lack of vulnerability I had in my heart surfaced, and I felt so heavy and confused. I knew

I had to have this conversation with him, but it was terrifying. Aunt Lo and Uncle B were very supportive every step of the way. They met me right where I was and helped me navigate everything with scripture and love.

Uncle B urged me to call him ASAP. He told me to call him the next day. Suddenly I remembered he was taking his dissertation exam that day. My Uncle looked at me and said, "Call that brother on Tuesday!" So, of course, leading up to this point, I was going through it. I had so many thoughts in my mind about how I knew he was probably just blowing me off, so I went to his Instagram page just to see if he was MIA on there. Yes, I am guilty of lurking. It looked to me as if this guy was having a blast. So at that point, I was like, what!? So, you are supposed to be busy and stressed out, but you're having fun!? I instantly got a little upset and told myself I wasn't calling. I talked to Uncle B a little that night, and he snapped me out of it. There was no way I was getting out of this conversation.

As you can see, my pride had me in a chokehold. Without the support I wouldn't have been able to take this step. I was praying ALL day at work. Being the over-thinker I am, I planned to call him as soon as I made it home. I walked through the door, spoke to my parents, and went straight upstairs to put my phone in a good spot for service. A dropped call for this conversation meant I might not even say what I had to say; yes, it was that difficult. I sat down in my room and calmed my spirit so to be as natural as possible. He has been my friend for a while now; it has never been difficult to talk to him. Knowing that didn't make this any more accessible, but it was too late, I had already pressed the call button.

The phone rang once, and he answered. It looks like those prayers had this timing thing right on point. He rarely answers the phone, period; forget the first ring. To think that was a surprise just as he was answering the phone, I saw my laptop buzzing; he was Face Timing me! All I could think was Lord Jesus take the wheel. A conversation I thought would be shielded by our distance was taken to another level. I thought this wouldn't be that bad, mainly because I was not right in front of him, but oh, that wasn't the case. I could see him, and the worst part was that he could see me. Darn you technology!

I started the conversation by asking him about his exam. As the conversation about school and work ended, I knew it was time for me to tell him. There is no cookie-cutter way to start an awkward conversation, so I went with the most cliché; "I called you because there is something that I wanted to talk to you about." Then he said to me, "You're pregnant!" I was so shocked that he would think I would call him and tell him that I was pregnant, so I played along. He gave me this horrified look and was like, for real!? Baffled by his shenanigans, I yelled NO! I asked him why he would think I would call and tell him something like that. He said, "I don't know; you could have named him after me." His antics lightened the mood, and I was able to flow into the conversation. My heart was beating like that moment right before the class presentation I didn't prepare for. I told him everything the best way I knew how, from our initial reunion to all confirmations. It wasn't until then did he realize that I was speaking about him. The response I got from him was a little different than I imagined.

After he initially deciphered through everything, he became aloof. At some point or another in the conversation, he asked how long we had known each other. Then he said to me, "So you mean to tell me that I have liked you for almost seven years, seven whole years, and you are just now telling me this?" I chuckled, and he said, "You're laughing, but I just want to, ugh!" He told me that if God was showing him, I was his

56

wife, he would have taken it and ran with it. He gave the example of Hosea. "God told him to marry a prostitute. Can you imagine God saying that to anyone? If God were showing me you, gorgeous Aria, I would be like, okay, God!" It was at that moment that I realized he was displeased.

He expressed how frustrated and conflicted he was. I felt in my spirit that for sure there was someone else. This didn't give me the warm fuzzies, but I felt such a relief with telling him everything that it didn't bother me as much as it typically would have. After an almost six-hour conversation I was drained. He went on to tell me the reason he was feeling so conflicted was that there was someone else. I will never forget him saying, "I still want to see where things go with this other girl." That one kind of hurt. At that point, I wanted to just get off the phone. I did my part; I put myself out there only to have my feelings hurt. What could I do about where he stood? Absolutely nothing but move forward in faith. I also expressed my frustration in how he just had this whole speech about what he would have done if he were me, but then went on to tell me that he still wanted to see where things went with this other person. Just that summer, we talked about how there is no such thing as dating, and when God presents your wife, you trust him.

As he continued to talk, I began to feel restless, but something inside of me—The Holy Spirit kept screaming, be selfless, allow him this time. Towards the end of our conversation, he received a revelation of why I brought everything to him. The Holy Spirit showed him that it isn't what I said, but that I needed to say it. He then received revelation for himself. The Lord showed him that he was acting and then asking God for his approval instead of seeking him first. He thanked me for being obedient, then said he would be spending some time with the Lord about everything. This conversation was disheartening and redemptive all at the same time. I was mainly happy with the milestone I reached by initiating it.

The morning after, I reached out to Aunt Lo and Uncle B to tell them how the conversation went. They were very supportive. Uncle B had a little more in mind than just giving me encouraging words. He said, "Go and see him". In shock, I replied, "Really?!" He calmly said, "Don't you want to?" All I could say was yes. The only thing on my mind was how he totally swerved my previous request and then told me he was exploring relations with someone else. I couldn't just say I wanted to come again, but I did. I didn't see the harm in going down, so here goes another pride hurdle, and after a somewhat frustrating conversation, we put a date on the calendar. I had to go back and forth with him about if he needed to study, he could and that I could entertain myself. God must have put a grace blindfold over my eyes because my swerve radar is so strong. Any other day I would have done just like before and said okay, maybe next time. But this time, I didn't, and the result was me driving to see him that next weekend.

I had a mixture of emotions. I was so excited just to see him and spend time, but what if it was weird? He didn't seem to want me to come. When I got there, he greeted me the same way he did when we saw each other for the first time in Tally. He embraced me, picked me up, and spent me around in excitement. We went up to his place and caught up a little. Everything felt so natural and genuine. That night he decided to cook, and we rode his motorcycle to the store for what he needed. When we got there, we ran into one of the girls I remembered competing against in college and another one of his friends I met during my first visit to Tallahassee. It was wonderful to see her again. You know you have met a genuine person when your encounter is just as enjoyable the second time around. Unknowingly she made my trip start to feel warmer.

After leaving the store, we went back to the house; he cooked, I watched, we talked, and then watched a little TV before bed. Him being a gentleman, he asked me how I felt comfortable sleeping. I remembered visiting him for the very first time when he was in school at Bama. We slept in the same bed, and it was like sleeping next to my brother. Well, I'm not sure if two extra-long twin beds pushed together counts as one bed, but hey, the principle still applies. I never felt uncomfortable with him in that way. I sometimes think as believers we get so tied up in this whole purity thing that we lose our minds. Granted, I feel it's beautiful to know yourself and personal boundaries, but can we really say it's biblical? Ruth went and laid at the foot of Boaz's bed, and she didn't even know him! Please don't go and do that. The moral of this story is many times we try to create biblical principles that are truly our own biases.

The next day he was supposed to get up to study, but instead, he randomly asked if I could be dressed in 30 min. I said yes, where are we going? He said, "Wherever God takes us!" and before I knew it, we were off on his bike. The weather was perfect. I felt so safe with him, even on his dangerous speed bike. As we were riding for about 10-15 min, we stopped in an open lot. Of course, because I wasn't aware of the plans, I thought maybe we were going for a walk. He asked me had I ever driven a bike before; I said, No. In my mind saying, I know you aren't thinking what I think you're thinking. Of course, he says to me in his Mr. Miyagi voice, "Well, you learn today."

My mouth dropped; I was so nervous. I had NEVER driven a bike before. He started slowly teaching me the basics of the bike. Initially, I just sat on the bike; then, I walked with it. I walked and put my feet up, and then my feet were up until I was giving the bike gas! I never went out of first gear, but the experience was liberating.

After we got back on the bike, he took me to a lake. It was so beautiful, the sun shining through the clouds onto the water. As soon as we got off the bike, a little girl ran over and asked us to play very assertively. Of course, me being the kid lover I am, I couldn't say no. We watched her play on the monkey bars for a little, then walked towards the lake. As we were walking, there was a little boy who yelled out, Hi guys! He couldn't have been older than 3 or 4. It was like our friendship was being accepted by innocence. It was like the universe was aligned, as a coach of mine used to say. Everything just felt right. I hope that when we are married, our life will reflect that day, quality time spent while embracing and celebrating others around us. I hope our love will bless and cultivate everyone around us as we pull strength from our union.

After quietly enjoying the scenery, we had a moment of goofiness. We took a few silly pictures and then headed back to the house. When we got back, he went to study, and I spent a little time to myself cuddled up on the couch. While relaxing, I received a random phone call from my childhood best friend, the same friend I spent that Labor day with at the zoo. We talked about life and how much we were grateful for our friendship. I told her who I was with, and she reminded me of her conversation with me a while ago about acting on everything God was showing me. She said, "See, this is what happens when you act." I love that girl dearly; we have been friends since diapers. She has a particular drive about life where she so easily removes her emotions when something needs to be said; it's admirable.

As we were ending our conversation, he was getting back to the house. That night we were supposed to go out, but we stayed in. The following day we went out for breakfast, and I planned to leave around noon. Breakfast was excellent, we talked about God, and he opened up about some spiritual things he was experiencing. I was able to see a different side of him. We talked about life and some of his future goals. I remember thinking about how we learned some new things about each other during the trip, but we never once talked about anything in relation to ourselves. I did tell him over the phone that I wouldn't mention it again—what the Lord had spoken to me about him. I didn't want him to feel pressured. God showed him to me, not the other way around. It seemed like the trip was only meant for us to learn a little more about each other. We talked a bit more when we made it back to the house, and I packed my things. He mentioned me just staying a little longer, and it felt reassuring. I could have taken that to be more endearing than it was, though.

After making it back home, I felt confused about what to do next. I wanted to talk to him consistently. I wanted to see him every once in a while, but I didn't know if he wanted the same or if God even wanted it. Aunt Lo encouraged me to keep the communication going. I had already been thinking about writing him a letter, so I thought this was perfect timing. Thanksgiving was that next weekend, so I wanted to tell him why I was thankful for him and what a great time I had. From the time I made it back home, and for about two weeks straight, our communication was pretty consistent until he was in a bike accident the night before my birthday. I didn't hear from him the entire day. I was hurt. I couldn't wrap my mind around how he could just forget, or maybe not even forget, but just not care. The day after he explained everything. The feeling I had in my stomach was unexplainable. I just wanted to be there. In the accident, he broke his phone, and I haven't heard from him since. I'm not sure if it's because his phone is still broken, or he has lost the desire to keep in touch. I have texted and called him, and nothing. Is this what he felt all those years I wasn't interested? All I can do now is pray and keep God as my center.

When I say pray, I mean praying in the spirit and not my understanding because I don't understand anymore. I have realized that faith means to move, so I moved and made myself vulnerable numerous times and was very much willing to do it again, but now my thoughts stop at thoughts with no resolve, and the question marks are there. I only know in my heart that he is my husband, but I don't know how or when this will genuinely be manifested. As you follow along in these chapters, this journey is one that you see everything unfold as I am. This short part of my journey has made me realize how often we can miss God from our ideology of what we think he would have for us to do. The whole time I was allowing things to drift away. I thought God wanted me to wait for him to reach out to me randomly. Don't allow yourself to get mixed up in the rules man creates. Allow God to lead your path, and no one else. There is no such thing as Christian dating. Certain principles are good to take from those guidelines, but you can't live your life by man's direction. Man didn't create the plan or the path.

The Hunt

As I have been on this journey trying to navigate life, I am very proud of how I can know and interact with someone God has shown me is my husband, and not get lost in that. My inner yearning is to give myself to God, and each time He shows me why He needs me as a vessel. I am overwhelmed and honored all at the same time. I am not worthy of having His words flow through me. During this journey, I have had to try so much in this situation. I have felt recently that I am doing so much to get him to see who I am, and it's very apparent that he isn't there. He doesn't see me, and it hurts. If it were anyone else, I would take it as a loss and move on; but because it's him, it hurts all the more, to know your future husband doesn't see or want you.

I ask myself questions like, when will things be different. Was what I felt about us being married by 2020 real? Was what Uncle B said about a year and a half the time it would take for him to see? Did I tell him or go down there at the wrong time? I don't know, and frankly, I don't care anymore. I have learned that it is not my job to navigate life for him and respond to various situations. I have to stay on the path that my GPS is on. I can't steer the wheel on my car and then hop in the front seat of someone else's. He is on his path, and God will show him what he needs to see. Our roads will meet at some point. Our paths have crossed at specific times before, but only at the right time will we merge onto the same route. God never wants us to lose our car and hop into the front seat with our spouse. You can pick up many more people along the way if you have more room in your vehicle. As a married couple, God makes the two one but He never intends for you to lose your identity, and the unique things that make you, well you. You have something this world needs; don't deprive others of it.

Last night I had a bad dream. The Lord placed me in the body of a person who has experienced much trouble in her life. This person was afraid, alone, and unprotected. Her mother did everything she possibly could to be a good mother and take care of her, but she was forced into some situations against her will. The daughter had to watch her mom go through so much. The mother did everything she could to wipe it all away, but the damage was done. In the dream, the Lord used my mother and me; it was so surreal. I felt EVERY feeling this young girl felt, EVERY sense. I felt alone and afraid. I felt like every man that walked too close was out to get me. It was so hurtful, but as I woke up, the Lord began to show me someone that my brother spoke about briefly a few days prior. I had to text him to see if he knew anything of detail about her past. When my brother called me that morning, I told him I wasn't sure who this person was, and he said to me, I do. I have not been able to sleep for two nights, and the Lord just kept showing me her face. My whole body went numb, and all I could do was cry again. I felt this flood of things that the Lord wanted to say to her. My heart was so grieved for her, and although this time passed, I know there is something that God has for her. We go about our everyday lives hearing stories about what people go through, but we never really know. At this moment, I learned never to forsake people's journeys. We don't know the depths of their hearts unless God shows us; we are only called to love.

This dream was a reminder to stay focused. Stay focused on the prize, and let everything else fall into place. In my heart, I desire to get to know my husband before the time we are married, but

none of that is essential. God has shown me why it is so important to know who you are in him before becoming one with someone else. God does not want you to lose your blueprint. If His only desire was for you to be a husband or a wife, you would have just come here that way. There is a reason why you live your life separate and become whole in God first. Without knowing and truly understanding this lesson, I could have missed this essence if I awakened love too soon. I trust God so much. He can do so much more than any human is capable of.

In this process, all I could think about were stories in the Bible where women were called to act! There are not many stories of women in the Bible, but the two that have stood out through this journey are Esther and Ruth. Esther was called to go and be a maidservant for the King. During that time, her people were in bondage. She was sent by faith to save them. She had no idea what would happen, but she lived, moved, and kept her being in Christ. Through her placement in the palace, the guard favored her. In the story, the king and his wife disagree. Queen Vashti upsets the King by her disobedience, and he instantly removes her and asks for another woman from the maidservants (Esther 2:17). Of the maidservants, Esther is chosen. Esther knew when she was being called out that it was her time. No one around her may have known what was going on, but she did. The Lord didn't just want to make her a Queen to sit on a throne and look pretty. He called her because she had work to do. Her union with the King meant so much more than just a union; it was meant to redeem.

Even in writing this passage, the Lord showed me, see, only Esther knew, just as you know. You know my will, and you are willing to do what it takes to see it manifest. 12.13.17

During this time, I have had difficulties feeling as though people didn't understand me or approve of what God was showing me. The Lord reminded me of Ruth and how she was instructed to go! Ruth obeyed and did the unthinkable. She worked hard in the field, picking up after the women picking the harvest and only taking leftovers. As she was doing so, she was favored in the eyes of the King. He fed her and allowed her to take home grain to her mother-in-law Naomi. Naomi instructed her to go back and find Boaz and, when he slept, to see where his feet were and lay there. This was Ruth acting on her faith. From Ruth's selfless actions, she had a son whom she named Obed. He was the father of Jesse, who was the father of David. Neither one of these women knew what would happen to them as they acted in faith, but as you can see, their love was for a bigger purpose, and when God intentionally brings two people together, you don't know the fruits that are intended to come from the union. Understand that even when it seems as though it is about you, it almost never is.

71

You Think You Know, but You Have No Idea

Towards the end of the last chapter, I thanked the Lord for revelation. The Lord had me study revelation and people in the Bible that He had given revelation to. He wanted me to look at each situation in detail and dissect it. As I started to do that, I had another encounter with Uncle B. He didn't know that up until this point, I hadn't heard from my friend. It has been about three weeks now since we last spoke. He was distraught when he heard. I was honestly at a point where I didn't care. This was too much work; I was all gassed out. He continued to tell me that love gives even when you don't want to, but my heart couldn't receive it. I felt like he didn't understand. I called Aunt Lo that same night. Her voice was always so soothing. Because her life experiences were very similar to mine, I felt like she would understand exactly how I was feeling. She told me to ask the questions I wanted to know the answers to. She said, "I want to know when people started feeling like they shouldn't ask questions they want to know answers to." Hearing it put so plainly, I agreed with her, so I called. I was a little upset that he answered the phone. That meant his phone was working again, and he didn't even bother to reach out. Aunt Lo encouraged me that no matter what, to ask the questions I needed and wanted to ask, so I did just that. I wanted to know why he didn't reach out to me even though we talked consistently before. Did he not like talking to me? Did he prefer I not reach out to him? It seemed as though he was shocked that I was even asking those questions. He reassured me that he had just been busy. I told him that being busy isn't the issue, but not communicating is. He apologized for my frustration in his absence, and we began to talk more often.

Although we were talking again, things still seemed weird. During this time, I remembered the Bible study the Lord placed on my heart. I mapped out everything I wanted to research but never researched it. Studying God's word brings to life things you would never think of. I started by defining Revelation and Prophecy. Revelation is a disclosure of truth or instruction. Prophecy is the gift of communicating and enforcing revealed truth or revelation. It is used to uplift the soul (mind, will, and emotions). Then, I began to look at different people God gave the word to and how they responded in the Bible.

Did they obey, did they listen instantly, or do their own thing? How did their decisions affect their lives? As I read, I found some common themes. The word would always come directly from God, an angel, or a prophet. When they first heard the phrase, they were many times afraid. They had doubts, asked questions, and then they made a decision. They decided whether they believed what God said. As I was reading, I ran across Luke 1:37 (NIV) as the birth of Jesus and his cousin John were being prophesied, the word said that God's word would never fail. It was like those words were burned on my heart, and I knew for the very first time without a doubt that what God was showing me was real. After spending so much of my time writing this book, you would think that I should have believed way before now. Instead, my thoughts were unstable and wavering because I wasn't standing on anything. I wasn't standing on the confirmation of God's word.

The same night I started my study on 12.20.17, I went to Bible study, and the pastor talked about standing on God's promises and gave us the tools to navigate it. This was total confirmation for me. On the way home from Bible study, I was quiet, and my brother asked why. Some comments were made at dinner from Uncle B about me getting to know a specific person. One of the only things I could think about when people would urge me to move away from what God was showing me, was Abraham and Hagar. Me pursuing a relationship with another man would essentially be a result of my unbelief. God doesn't waste his breath. When He confirms Himself, and rest assured He does, stand on that. In the conversation with my brother, I told him how I was going back and forth about visiting my friend again. It was on my heart to go down when one of my former students would be in town for a game against the Seminoles. Of course, Julius made the gestures seem so simple. I exclaimed how when the Lord guided Ruth to sleep at Boaz's feet, he didn't kick her off the bed after he saw her. I felt like my revelation was being rejected. My story wasn't looking right. He stopped me and said, what if all of this is explicitly about you. Well, of course, it is. He was right, I needed to say something about coming to visit. That next day I reached out and he agreed.

Your Faith Will Be Tested

After knowing I was going to Tally for a visit, I felt a certain happiness in my heart, regardless of what my mind was trying to get me to believe. I had a trip scheduled to go to Miami the weekend of Christmas to spend some time with my sister-in-law and her family, and I was looking forward to the time away. Of course, during this time, it crossed my mind that I may have run into the guy from my past, but with everything inside of me, I wanted to avoid him. I knew from how long it took me to move past everything we went through before I needed to keep my distance. Of course, since my life is such a movie, guess who I ran into? When I got there, I connected with a great friend, who I met through my high school best friend from Miami. They both were in town, so we decided to go out that night. My brother and sister-in-law were also supposed to come but decided not to. We were eager to spend some time together, so we continued with our plan to hit a Caribbean birthday celebration. I can't begin to tell you how much I love island music, and always have even from childhood. Whenever I hear it being played, I feel this overwhelming sense of belonging. I remember showing a beautiful soul who I met through my connect group a picture of me on the beach in the Bahamas. She said to me, you look like you belong, in her Jamaican accent. She didn't know I shared her sentiment.

Anyway, we are out, and not five minutes go by before my friend looks at me and says, "Aria, Aria." I didn't want to hear what was coming after that because I knew what she was going to say. He was there. I didn't even want to look in his direction, but after seeing him pace around the party, I knew it was insane and a little immature to try to ignore him the entire night. So I looked in his direction and waited for him to notice me. When we made eye contact, he had this bemused look on his face. I smiled at him briefly, and he just gazed back. I didn't know if he would speak to me, but I wasn't trying to figure that out. I hadn't talked to him in months. I blocked his number because I felt like I needed to remove myself and move on. It was so awkward seeing him. He could have either been really upset with me or possibly even on a date, but I was wrong; he finished the conversation with his friends and walked over to me.

We began to talk out feelings that were left unsaid. It was one of the most balanced disagreements we have ever had. We agreed that a lot of our final conversations were misunderstandings and apologized for feelings hurt. I didn't think there would be much more interaction from that moment, but I was wrong. We talked quite a lot at the party, considering we weren't there together. With each encounter, I became more comfortable with him, just almost like the progression of our relationship. It's kind of like the enemy comes at us in spurts until we get comfortable. I hate using similarities from this relationship to things like that, but if God has shown me someone else, this can't be much more than a distraction, right?

That night he wanted to talk more, and I agreed. We talked about how he offered to stay with him in Miami before I left, but I never brought the conversation up again. I mean, he knew I was leaving but never once clearly asked me if I would stay. I am almost sure I would have, even if it were only for a month. When thinking of that, I knew that was why my efforts to stay in Miami were so unsuccessful. I had fallen deeply in love with him and was willing to do whatever it took to be close to him comfortably. The situation didn't end that way, but what if it had? What could I be ruining? The decisions we make cause chain reactions that we often don't realize the effects of until it's too late. I mean, look at how easy it was for me to fall back into a particular place with someone I know God didn't say was my husband. If things had flowed differently with him, meaning it was a healthy relationship, I wouldn't have known how to move on without a push from God. Heck it was toxic, and I didn't know how to move on.

This is exactly why God never intends for us to date around; there is no biblical truth to dating. I am genuinely drawn to this man, but he isn't for me regardless of how much I try to make him. We parted ways that night, and I became a bottle of confusion.

That encounter opened the door to a miserable position that I put myself in. This is a prime example of what it looks like when we detour to paths God never intended for us to travel. That next day I was expecting to see him as planned from our conversation the night before, and he never followed through, per usual. Flashbacks of disappointment were so real. This was a reminder that this person hasn't changed.

79

Surprisingly that same day, I got an unexpected phone call from my "old friend". He had a very different tone; it was slightly odd. He was talking about his communication and how he knew it was terrible. It felt like suddenly everyone had wake-up calls, and I was getting tossed in the waves of my emotions. I traveled back home, and the consistency continued, but the interruption of rekindling with my old friend caused what would have usually been excitement in my heart to feel numb. I knew then that he was the reason for many distractions; even as I type these words, I feel tempted to go back to what is familiar.

The Devil doesn't tempt you until you are lacking something. There is no way I would have even entertained the thought of this person if I was secure in everything God has given me. The Devil tempted Jesus with bread right as he was finishing his fast. He was hungry, and the enemy knew. It took me a minute to move forward, but I did.

When a person's efforts are enough to get you to let your guard down, they soon show their true colors. No one can ever fit the shape of something else for too long. It's kind of like the scripture, James 4:6-12 that my friend and I studied one morning while I was visiting. The scripture speaks about not being able to have bitter and sweet water flowing from the same well. What is inside of a person will always come out. That's why it's essential when you meet people to give time to get to know them before any conclusions are drawn.

The Lion's Den
1.11.18

Last week was the last time I would initiate a trip to see my friend in Tally. My younger cousin came along as well to catch up with friends of hers who attend the university. During my ride there, I kept noticing how beautiful the clouds were. I wrote an entire blog on Grace to Ari about how I love clouds and always have since childhood. I believe God sends me little "I love you notes" through clouds. Each moment of my drive was breathtaking. The clouds were like nothing I had ever seen before. Their texture looked like a bunch of cotton balls stacked up on top of each other that had been polished and shined to perfection. Then as the sun began to set, the colors were so immaculate. There was one cloud that a rainbow was coming down from. The grass was greener than grass I had ever seen, and it was winter! I could feel the beauty of everything around me deep down in my soul. I felt the Lord was showing me the beauty and significance of this trip. He was showing me that my universe was aligned.

Once I got there, my friend was busy studying as we were attending the basketball game. After I dropped my cousin off, I headed to the house to see him. He came down when I arrived but was focused on covering his motorcycle. The vibe I was getting from him was a little blah, so instantly, my mood changed. At that moment, I noticed how much I allow other people's actions to dictate my response. He said to me, are you tired? I can feel your tiredness from here. I was exhausted, but more importantly I wanted him to greet me as he normally would. You know, pick me up and spin me around all fairytale-like. I got picked up all right. Picked up and thrown over his shoulder like a rag doll. Nevertheless, he was still his joking self, and I warmed up. When we got to his place, I put my things down, and we chatted a bit about the day. I am always so tired after a road trip. I took a shower, relaxed a little, and fell asleep. It's something different about when I'm close to him. My soul feels at rest. I have said this before as it pertains to other people, but I see now that it was always a façade. With him my heart never feels like it's unprotected; even with the uncertainty of

83

this situation. I don't ask him questions about other women because I know they are non-factor. My father's word will never return void.

1.29.18

It was and always has been him. As I find myself wanting to veer from the course because of what I see, I am reminded that it has always been him. In moments where I feel all is lost, he is there. The capacity is many times different, but he is always there. I write today in a place of doubt because of what I see. But I still trust my God for whatever happens. My suspicion does not understand how there will be a transformation taking place while feeling the inability to try. I have, in so many ways, stepped outside of myself to show my heart, and it was never reciprocated. When you see someone show that they can put forth effort as it pertains to romance, but just not with you, it hurts. Many times in life, I have walked into situations hoping that a specific time would be different, hoping I wouldn't get heartbroken, and I did. I could feel it, but I couldn't see it coming. In this situation, I know what the Lord is showing me, but I see the opposite. In the other cases, I knew it wasn't right, but I still hoped for different. With my friend, I know it's real, but because I don't see a change, I count it out. This situation isn't tangible. I know what God showed me, but as far as this situation goes, I don't know what to think or feel. I am all out of energy, and there is not an inch of desire in me to try. I have been hurt so many times in my life. I realize marriage is about giving; however, I have nothing else to offer. After being in situations where you give and give of yourself, hoping they will see your heart and they never do, the disappointment becomes a reality you never want to experience again. But nevertheless, you do, again and again, each time hoping that things would be different.

The common denominator here isn't that men have continued to hurt me. The common factor is that I have allowed myself to fall for someone just because they showed intent interest. I have called myself "going with the flow" until the flow never stopped, and I found myself compromising the one thing that really means the world to me. So here I am, with the man who my Father says is for me, and he doesn't even see me that way. That is a hard reality to face, but I push and continue to crack out of this shell of my old self until I am completely exposed and made new.

Doubting Debbie
2.1.18

Have you ever wondered why the book of Psalms is such a well-known book of the Bible? I think it's because it appeals and speaks directly to our emotions. Not many books in the Bible express the emotional, physical, and mental state of a person the way the Psalmist does in Psalms. The truth is no one really wants to talk about tough times while they are going through them, but David clearly did. A lot of his writings were in the present tense. When you are going through it and can write about it real time it's authentic. Most books are written after everything occurs. This particular journey has been pretty arduous. Writing has been the furthest thing from my mind, but I felt the Holy Spirit nudging me to write.

I have been hearing the Lord say to me you need to write, so here it is. During the time when my old friend and I were in contact, there was a sense of underlying happiness, but after this most recent trip, I have realized that I got a little too passionate about being a doer. Yes, faith without works is dead, but you can operate within your own might and start to go before God, trying to help him. This has been something that I have always done in other aspects of life. I have never applied it in relationships, so I didn't see myself. I realized God wanted me to activate my faith by sharing my heart and making an effort to spend some quality time, but you can't force a person to desire you. I noticed our communication was pretty dry, and I initiated for him to visit Georgia to go hiking, and well, I was pretty much swerved—again. I think I am relatively passive in a way naturally. If someone is showing me they have no interest, I have no problem with giving them space. It's not that I won't try, but if things aren't working, they just aren't working.

I feel that I am in a peculiar and vulnerable place where I have begun to doubt the process of the manifestation of God's word for me. I just don't see it anymore, and maybe it isn't for me to see. I find myself wanting to just live my life for what it is, not worrying about tomorrow or what it may bring. I do realize that place has specific parameters, but I will be very transparent and say that this place spoke to my flesh. I began to have flashes of myself just enjoying life, being careless, and engaging in sexual sin. I didn't allow myself to stay in that place or to act on it, but just going there in my thoughts was so unhealthy spiritually. I had to repent and really ask God for his forgiveness. God showed me that when life isn't going my way, I throw an adult tantrum.

God sees our end before the beginning. He knows when we engage in the enemy's traps, we open ourselves up to be deeply hurt; mentally, physically, and spiritually. I think if we understood that life isn't about God stopping us from doing things, we think are fun, it would change the dynamic of how we walk. God wants to stop us from the pseudo-fun. That fun we think is fun but will have you crying your eyes out later. Fun that will bring so much hurt, you have to make life changes just to align your soul again. Fun that leads to depression and whatever else sin can buy these days.

God loves us so much he wants to shield us from those types of things. The devil comes to steal, kill, and destroy (John 10:10). I think we take this scripture too lightly. Go back and just read those words. How would you feel about a person who was stealing from you, trying to kill you, or people close to you, and ultimately striving to destroy you? If you knew someone like this, would you keep them around? I think we linger because he always comes bearing gifts. Gifts that look like a diamond ring but will really turn your finger green. I realize the place I am in, and this time around, I am going to put forth more effort to stay aligned. I don't know what will happen next, and I can't say I am trying to figure it out. I'm so tired. All I can do is trust in God and believe in his word. Everything else will just have to fall into place.

After writing earlier this week, I was really starting to feel like myself again. So much so that I felt the urge to text my friend from Miami. I told him that us just being friends was the best thing and that I would always love him. Why did I do that? He then invited me on a ski trip, and although it didn't sit well after we spoke about it in detail, it was appealing to underlying desires I had been harboring, so I said yes. I purchased my ticket to go and even started to buy a few items I needed for the trip. This was the most bittersweet vacation I had ever planned. In one breath, I am thinking about how much I wanted to stay in a place of purity, but on the flip side, I was so familiar with this person that I knew realistically speaking it was possible for me to compromise my walk. I allowed what I knew in my heart to be suitable to fade with my desire for companionship. I let my flesh make the decision in this situation.

Just hold on

2.21.18

Usually, when you are planning a fun getaway, the moments leading up feel fun and fulfilling because you have something to look forward to. Just yesterday, I was on my way home from work, which is about an hour and a half drive. At times I find myself all out of options to entertain myself, so I just ride in silence. My thoughts keep me consumed sometimes, and they aren't always conducive to my progress in life. Nevertheless, I was thinking, and I remembered thinking to myself, maybe this is all in my head speaking of everything I felt the Lord was showing me. For the first time in a while, that set well with me. It was like an "oh well" feeling. I went on about my day and forgot I ever said it.

That night as I was getting out of the shower, I went to put my clothes in the laundry room, and I noticed the hamper top was misaligned. I reached in to pull it out, and I found an infinity necklace that I thought I lost. I had been looking for it for so long that I forgot about it. I remember when I first got the chain. Someone noticed it and said, "Infinity, what does that mean to you?" Never-ending. They replied, "No, what does it mean to YOU." To me, the infinity necklace represents God's, never-ending love. Finding it made me feel as though God was sending me an "I Love You." He does that every once in a while when I need it the most, and it's always in a way that I know it's only Him. All I could do was smile. When life is hectic, and my emotions are all over the place, and God steps in to let me know that He loves me, it reminds me that it's just Him and I. It makes everything else in the world not so big when I feel God encasing me in His loving arms.

I finished everything I had to do for the night and went to bed. That night I had a dream that made me forget my current life status; it was so real. I dreamed of my wedding. In the dream everything was so chaotic. My mom was trying to talk to me, asking me did I know where something was, and my dad did something to make me upset. My best friend and brother were trying to console me, and my husband-to-be was nowhere to be found! Even in the dream, it never crossed my mind that he wasn't going to show. I knew that wasn't the case, so I FaceTimed him. As soon as he answered, I began yelling at him, wondering why he wasn't there. I remember seeing a little boy getting ready and him saying, I'm trying to get him ready; it has been hectic. I don't know who the little boy was, but I had never seen him before.

When we got off of the phone, I realized my hair was in this weird bun. I asked Nye why my hair looked like that, and she told me it was because I said he liked natural styles. I became more conscious about it and instantly wanted to change it. As we were changing my hair, he arrived and was waiting for me at the altar. While making last-minute changes, I heard my song que. I instantly panicked and told everyone to cut the song off and stall. I have to be beautiful I yelled! I remember as my Aunt Wanda was fixing my makeup. I was getting anxious and saying, please hurry, I don't want him to think I'm not coming. Weird dream, huh? Would you believe just the vision of marrying him gave me peace? The dream was the reminiscent of a nightmare, but because we are very distant now, even a nightmare gave me peace. If the thought of such a horrible chaotic wedding ceremony can bring joy, then what much more will everything be when it manifests the way God intended?

As I was getting ready this morning, I began to replay the dream in my head, and all I could think about were the two parts when one of us was ready, and the other wasn't. That feeling pretty much sums up our story thus far. I look forward to the day when we are both on the same page. This situation is so challenging, and some days I don't know what to do with it, but I just keep living my life as if it never happened.

2.23.18

After having the dream, I was still feeling a little off. That Friday night, I was getting my hair done. My hairdresser who I have been going to since high school, and is absolutely amazing, I might add, was trying to set me up with someone. He sounded great, and in my mind, I was like, why not. So I told her she could give him my number. That next day I remember feeling off, like something wasn't right, then came Sensei. My friend, who I spoke about at the beginning of the book who sat with me at dinner and confirmed a lot of the things I felt God was showing me about my journey. That day he sent me a text message with word from the Holy Spirit. The overall theme of the text was enough was enough. I was entertaining thoughts of being with other people and planning ski trips. The Lord said this is your burden to carry, not anyone else's. No one else has to believe but you.

I hoped at this moment that the guy my hairdresser was setting me up with wouldn't text, but he did. Initially, in our conversation, I contemplated just going out with him, but it didn't feel right. For the first time in a while, I listened to what I knew to be right in my heart regardless of what seemed to be harmless and messaged him, letting him know that I couldn't go out. Even that felt hard for me, and I hadn't even met him yet.

Later that day, I was doing laundry, and heard The Spirit speaking to me, saying, "Okay, so you called that one-off, but what about this trip?" I couldn't help but think of how I already bought my ticket. "I already made plans God; I can't just cancel it." How many times do we blow off the direction of the Holy Sprit for plans we "already" made?

That Sunday night, as I got ready for bed, I prayed earnestly to the father, saying, "Lord, if this trip is not one that you want me to go on, show me, and I will follow you, I will be *obedient*." I asked that He allow me to get my money back in some way, whether it is a credit or refund. My flight was non-changeable/non-refundable. Monday 2.26.18 I was driving to work, and I realized the entire weekend went by, and I hadn't heard from the guy I was going on the trip with. There were still some loose ends to our plans, and I found it odd that we hadn't spoken, so I contacted him.

He told me he had a family emergency and that he wasn't even thinking about the trip. This made me feel a certain heaviness in my heart, but I knew it was my way out. I called the airline, and they gave me credit for the trip. The trip was off. I was feeling super emotional after all of this. I knew it was for the best, but then I had to deal with the reality I was facing, and I didn't want to. I allowed doubt to almost conceive an Ishmael. I was going down a path that could have opened a door for my destruction. The truth of the matter is that your doubt doesn't change God's word. Your actions, as you allow doubt to fester only causes turmoil God never intends.

That day on my ride home, I had a conversation with a beautiful friend of mine, Tish, who I met through my brother when she came to Atlanta for a conference. I felt like I needed to vent, and she always listened. Talking to her reminded me that my mom dreamed of a wedding the week before around the same time that I did. When she initially told me I overlooked everything she was saying, not realizing that not only did we both dream of a wedding but someway certain parts of our dreams intersected. In my mom's dream, she couldn't find her shoe; I guess that is what she was looking for in my dream? She kept saying that before having this dream, I was heavy on her heart, and she was worried about me.

She said although I know you're living your life, you don't seem complacent. She went on to describe an arduous feeling in her dream of a weight. She said it was so heavy that when it was finally over, she could feel something had been lifted, something shifted. She said the Holy Spirit spoke and said, "It won't happen until I say so." I asked my mom if she desired for me to be married soon? She told me no; she knew everything would happen when it was supposed to.

I knew when she said the Lord was showing her the weight I felt that He showed her because of her deep concern for what I was experiencing. Throughout the journey, I have many times felt like people don't really understand what I'm going through. To be a person that is close to family and not have one person understand hurts a little. It meant a lot to feel my mom connect with my feelings with the Lord allowing her to see and feel my heart so clearly.

Everything just felt like too much, like I was having a breakdown. All of these instances made me feel a sense of chaos in my spirit, coupled with transition. There was something in me that just wanted to make a change and completely indulge myself in the Lord. I began to long for that feeling of contentment that I had before knowing any of the things that we're currently causing confusion in my life. Back then, nothing could have moved me from where I was. I wanted to be nowhere else than abiding in God's love. Right here, right now, I am so exhausted with life and trying to foist things on my own. It's like God showed me something, and I just ran with it without waiting for instruction. Maybe if I was focusing on God the way I should, then He would have space to give me direction. I feel like I've been running wild, not knowing if this decision or that decision was right or wrong. God will never bring any of his children into a situation of pure chaos.

Looking Back on Himself

Snatched Back into Territory

3.13.18

Looking back on everything, God really did save me from myself. Every day I felt myself wishing I was going on that ski trip. I had to remind myself that God was protecting me from something I was oblivious to. Since then, I have focused more on God. I began to attend church more consistently. In doing so, I realized my actions recently had much deeper meaning. I was looking for self-fulfillment in things other than God. I was looking for it through relationships. I was reminded that there is no fulfillment in this earth better than God. Can you imagine that? If you really allow God to penetrate your entire being the way He desires, it means so much more than any fleshly desire can fulfill. My unbelief made way for sin, but God stopped me; rather He protected me. I just want to follow God's will for my life as I dig up all these roots seeded in my heart that render brokenness. We have always to realize the root cause of why we do things, and then dig it all the way out. Cutting the tree at the surface still leaves room for the roots to grow.

Drought in the Desert
4.2.18

As I have been allowing God to work out some things in my heart, I have made conscious efforts not to think too far ahead on things I can't control. I don't know when I will get married, but because God has shown me who my husband is, it's hard not to think ahead. If I have learned anything in this journey it would be not to try and fill in the rest of the puzzle before He gives you the rest of the pieces. I have found myself doing that many times with this situation, and it only gives me anxiety which Matthew 6:34 says explicitly not to do.

I remember watching a TV show where an inmate told someone that hope was a dangerous thing, one of the most challenging things he could do. I found myself agreeing with that statement. The Holy Spirit reminded me that faith is the substance of things hoped for. Faith is the fuel we need for those things we are hoping for Hebrews 11:1-39. Describing this passage of scripture doesn't do it justice so I must cite at least verses 1-8:

1 Now faith is the substance of things hoped for, the evidence of things not seen.

2 For by it, the elders obtained a good report.

3 Through faith, we understand that the worlds were framed by the word of God so that things that are seen were not made of items that do appear.

4 By faith, Abel offered unto God a more excellent sacrifice than Cain, by which he obtained witness that he was righteous, God testifying of his gifts: and by it, he being dead yet speaketh.

5 By faith, Enoch was translated that he should not see death; and was not found, because God had translated him: for before his translation he had this testimony, that he pleased God.

6 But without faith, it is impossible to please him: for he that cometh to God must believe that he is and that he is a rewarder of them that diligently seek him.

7 By faith Noah, being warned of God of things not seen as yet, moved with fear, prepared an ark to the saving of his house; by the which he condemned the world, and became heir of the righteousness which is by faith.

8 By faith Abraham, when he was called to go out into a place which he should after receive for an inheritance, obeyed; and he went out, not knowing whither he went.

I have never read this whole chapter until today, and my soul is so full of the goodness of God. This passage shows numerous deeds of faith. Each and every one of these people acted, and it was pleasing to God. Our faith moments on earth are only trinkets of the most significant reward faith can ever give, and that is eternal life. By faith, I made myself vulnerable at a time where there was no comfort in the reception of my heart. To this day, there hasn't been any manifestation of God's word. We know from many of these stories that there was a waiting period after they began to act; it didn't just instantly happen. So in this time;

I hope that someday soon, I will stop feeling this empty longing to see the manifestation of God's word,

I hope that our lives will be prosperous and fruitful,

I hope someday we will get the chance to know each other intentionally,

103

I hope that years don't pass, and my heart becomes sorrowful,

I hope that You hear and see my heart, Lord,

I hope You see that I'm trying so hard to keep it together

I hope You know that even when I get weary, the longing of my heart is to do Your will, and with all the hopes and dreams, I will lay them all aside for Your love and for Your choice...I will be still.

The Fight

This journey has been so enjoyable, but I find many people don't understand it. Often times in life, when you are going through trials, you seek people who will come into agreement with you. I do that frequently when I'm upset and trying to navigate life's crazy moments. In this situation, moments of reaching out to loved ones have felt much worse than just talking to God. I have been called to trust God no matter what I see. When the angel came to Mary, she chose to believe and obey God's direction. There had to be people who thought she was absolutely nuts. There were people who laid eyes on Jesus and still didn't believe. God's word doesn't need anyone's approval; as I quoted previously, He does whatever He pleases.

The beauty of Mary's obedience was that she could care less of what other people thought. Joseph was called to be the earthy father of Jesus, and he was like, nope. Mary, you slept around on me, and you think I'm going to be your husband? His plan was to divorce her quietly so to honor her. Most people would not have even done that; nevertheless, God still had a plan. He sent an angel to come to Joseph in his sleep, and from that encounter Joseph then knew truth. He responded accordingly thereafter (Matthew 1:18-25). When God is leading you to act on his word you don't have to worry about trying to direct other people. God has a handle on all things.

God's word never fails regardless of how we respond to it. It has been tough not having the people that are closest to me understand where I am. The few people that are standing in the agreement have been so encouraging in hard times. People who have stood and fought with me, even in my lowest moments. I feel the Lord has strategically placed certain people in my life for this purpose, and maybe even beyond. As I began to transition myself into really believing and taking hold of what God has shown me, I began to see myself as the lioness. Alone in the safari, under a tree. That tree represents God. He is my source of life. My covering, my hiding place, my refuge in a deserted land. That was where I saw myself in the last chapter, but now I see myself fighting—fighting against things that come my way to throw me off track. Everything that comes my way, I have to fight and be strong, but I see my strength, and it's bold. It's just my Father and I. He's all I've got, and He's all I need. This is not easy for me, and sometimes the thought of waiting years for any of this to manifest scares me, but I trust my God, and I know He knows best.

Many times when God is trying to grow our faith, He will use the very thing we put the most of our energy into to do it. Where our treasure is there will our heart will also be (Matthew 6:21). God knows that a woman's heart relationally is one of the most delicate parts of who she is. This is described in Genesis when He says that a woman will long for her husband (Genesis 3:16). I know God would never continuously bombard my life with this situation to then turn around and say, just kidding. I told you he was your husband, but he changed his mind hehe. Remember God's character when you are navigating the revelations He gives you. It is so vital when you live in a world where people have a ton of theories and opinions.

The Home Stretch

Things have felt difficult lately. It's like I got the energy and courage to fight, but just like anything that takes energy, at a certain point, you begin to get tired. Many times during this period, I have gotten discouraged, but for some reason, the discouragement is never enough for me to compromise, and I am proud of that. I want so much to be pleasing to God that just gratifying my flesh isn't enough, and I wouldn't have been in this place without His grace and mercy.

There are times during this part of my walk where I want to give up. It's scary that I find myself in those places, but when I wake up that next morning and realize I continued the race even if I was strolling, I am still moving forward. I may have been distracted in my thoughts, but I didn't allow myself to act. This is the point in my journey when it feels easy to give up and go back to what feels most comfortable. There isn't a lot of fun happening when you are growing spiritually. There can be a lot of lonely quiet times, but overall when you can get over the hard days, what's before you is that much more rewarding.

    I spoke earlier about my initial confirmations. During that time, I will never forget, one day, I was showering, I felt I heard the Spirit say, *"Give him two and a half to three years."* It was so subtle and sharp. I knew it didn't come from me because I wouldn't have given him any time if it were left up to me. I also didn't know whether or not it could be the enemy. After I reconnected with my old friend, it seemed as though things had moved along, but for some reason, *two and a half to three years* continued to come to the forefront of my mind. I began to pay attention to when the time frame was. I received the prophetic word as it pertained to him in August of 2015, exactly August 26, 2015, and I visited on August 27, 2015. I began to count, and the time frame just didn't make sense to me. Two and a half years from August was February of this year (2018). During that time, there was zero communication. I started to doubt what I was feeling in my spirit because nothing had come about in February. That left August; what would happen in August? I began to tell myself that God wouldn't give me a time frame. Why would God give me a time frame if he is all-knowing and knows the exact moment and time that we would move forward in the manifestation of his word? It just didn't make sense to me until recently.

After February passed, I began to tell myself that I obviously wasn't hearing from God if nothing happens by August of this year. So I began to have an expectation for that time frame somewhat while still wondering why God gave me a time frame to begin with. One day I was lying on my bed thinking about where I was and pondering on life. I thought about the last time I saw my friend and the time frame the Lord gave me, and subtlety, the Lord showed me the time frame was the time that he needed his time alone with God. It was his time to grow in the Lord in whatever way God saw fit, without my interference. From February to August is the time frame from two and a half years to three years. That was the essence of the time. That time frame is exactly six months until August. I received this revelation in May, and the Lord said to me, "I gave you a range because if I had just told you three years, you wouldn't have understood that the six-month period was very important." I was completely astounded. A little part of me began to see the time frame as a blessing. I began to somewhat see it as something that I could hold on to in this difficult time, but a little part of me doesn't want to hold on to it because I don't want to be anxious or disappointed if it doesn't happen the way I feel in my spirit it will.

I shared this revelation with Aunt Lo. We went to dinner on June 2, 2018, and she said something that really resonated in my spirit. She said, "You know with the things of God, people always think the blessing will come instantly, but with his promises, there is seedtime and harvest." I saw a vision of a small leaf coming out of the ground, like when a plant first starts to sprout. At that point of growth, you can see something is there, but you can rarely differentiate what type of plant it is until it begins to bear its fruit. I felt the Lord's word that night right before I traveled to Tally was the seed. Our conversations and my confirmations were the watering, and the distance and time I am dealing with now are our time to wait for the seed to continue to grow until our harvest; this is the wait.

As I write this revelation, the time period began to make even more sense. I remember writing in my journal about all of this. The place I was writing from was a place of frustration because of where I was. As I wrote, the time frame popped into my head, and for the very first time,

111

I wrote the dates down so that I could see them clearly. I wrote 2015 [2/2018 **or** 8/2018], and as I looked back at how that was written, it's a range! It isn't, **or** it's **between**! I wrote at the end of this journal entry that I didn't want to dwell on those dates, but I wouldn't forget them. This was on 2.26.2018. It was the same day my ski trip was canceled. Many times we think things are being taken away from us when God is giving us so much more back. I remembered thinking, "Wow, February is pretty much over, and if nothing happens in August, then surely I am making things up in my head. Today I was even overthinking and saying to myself, wait, what if he meant three years from the time I heard that in my spirit and not the time of our encounter? Which give or take was no more than a month later, and instantly the Holy Spirit said to me, "Now you don't do that. Don't allow yourself to take away the trinkets you have been given for overthinking. You know back when you heard that, you felt in your spirit it was from the time it was given to you." All I could do was laugh because I knew the enemy couldn't say that to me. I knew it was God because only God knows my thoughts and can respond to me so promptly. This was a key piece in learning how to navigate His voice. I used to convince myself that the enemy knew what I was thinking, but he didn't.

He is not omnipresent; he can only give you suggestions. He can't respond to your thoughts; only God can do that. God knows our thoughts a far off (Psalm 139:2).

A few months ago, my mom said she felt joy in her spirit that something was different, something good. I was feeling the same thing, and I felt like it was because I was entering into a new realm. God is just so good, and I am so thankful for every little thing He does to help give me encouragement on this long journey. I know I am different in so many ways, and I have grown so much. I find joy in the genuine love that other people discover for themselves. I can be around couples and not compare. I was going through an old phone back up the other day looking for a picture. I never found the picture, but I did find some old messages from that first year I met my old friend. My college roommate and I were planning a trip to visit, which surprise! It was August 26th, 2011.

Sometimes, when I am thinking back on the past, I ask myself, what if? What if I had responded to his gestures back when we were in college? What if I could have gotten over my immature idiosyncrasies? After going through all of those questions in my head, I realized that isn't at all what I wanted. I know that if I had gotten into a relationship at any point before, I wouldn't be the woman I am today. I would not have found the deeper parts of my solidarity with God. I wouldn't be the spiritually mature person I have grown to be. I wouldn't be the calmer and wiser version of myself. I deserve to know my creator intimately before I join a union, and he deserves that too. He deserves a woman that can hold her own spiritually, a woman that knows how to pray for him. He deserves a woman that is gentle and wise. He deserves a woman that can raise children in the admonition of the Lord and exemplify the traits women embody as creations of God. If at any point he and I had been together sooner, I wouldn't have gotten the opportunity to become the woman that I am. I might not have even been writing this book if I wasn't allowed that time to grow.

I get excited when I think about the blessing God has waiting for me. I have to keep telling myself it will come, it will come, and when it does, it's going to be glorious. I am going to tell the world. I am learning to wait patiently and contently. I have learned not to covet and to have joy in my own experiences with the Lord. Don't try to make the joy of others yours. This journey has been such a growth period, and I have just been walking and growing with Him. There has been so many wonderful things with my busines ventures and Unlimited. Even in this time, I have felt the Lord planning my wedding!

Yes, my wedding. That may sound so crazy, but God will involve Himself in any part of your life that you open to Him. I remembered walking out of my office at work and over to another building on campus, as I do most every day. There is a pathway that leads to the building. It's surrounded by trees, flowers, and beautiful chirping birds.

For some reason, every time I walk through that area, I feel the Lord's presence all over. One day I asked Him, why is it at this point of my day that I feel Your Spirit so strongly? He responded and said, "This is the way I would like for you to walk at your wedding." My heart leaped. He continued and said, "Count the steps." So I did; I counted 69 steps. I was so confused by those numbers; they didn't make sense; and literally, just as I am writing these words, the Lord showed me what they mean! 6 months represents the time frame we are in right now, February 2018 to August 2018—walking with God, growing and changing in our alone time with him, void of any distraction. The 9 represents the nine months until May of 2019, which is the revelation Uncle B received. Man, if all of this is made up, I am an absolute psycho, and if it's not, then it brings me total joy to know that God cares so much about my life and has made everything so perfect.

God has even shown me, bridesmaids. I have always told myself that I wanted a very small number of people. With these thoughts, and with each person on my mind that would not be a part of it, those relationships began to come around. Each time a friendship was reconciled, or a new one grew. I felt God showing me; certain people had to take part because of His glory. My wedding day is not meant to be private, the way I prefer for it to be. That would be like a person receiving a miracle and never telling anyone. I prayed that God would continue to help me plan my wedding. I'm not sure how any of this will go in reality, but my ultimate goal is always to be used by God every step of the way and for us to be selfless in this process.

It is such a blessing when God is in the center; He is so symbolic and purposeful. With everything He has shown me with this planning, I thought about the moments when God would instruct His people to do things. When He instructed Noah to make the ark, He gave him specific instructions. When he instructed Moses to build the Ark of the Covenant, he gave him specific instructions. When God told Joshua how the Israelites would conquer Jericho, He gave them specific instructions. Now He is doing it with me, but with my wedding! One of the most special days of a woman's life He is planning for me. It brings to life the consistent and never-changing nature of God. The more I grow and learn, the more I see that He is the God from before. He is the God that spoke to the prophets from long ago. He is the God of Abraham, Isaac, and Jacob. And my prayer is that God will continue to give me revelation and direction for my entire life. God's plan is a perfect plan. He knows exactly what we need when we need it.

The Wedding Planner

That Sunday as I sat on my grandmother's couch writing, the Lord continued to flood me with revelation. It was so much I was starting to feel a little crazy. I shared with Aunt Lo that for some time, I had been feeling like I needed to stop talking about this situation. Not that I had shared it with tons of people, but because of how discouraging it could be to share things that people don't understand, it just felt easier. After I made that decision, I began to walk in it; I began to get stronger. I wasn't allowing any little thing to trip me up. I didn't allow relationships that had no intentions of being just friends to fester. That used to be one of my biggest weaknesses. As I started to settle into the new place I journeyed to in my life, I began to feel the Lord nudging me to share this story with certain people. I don't speak about the place that I am in very much now, but there are times when I know I have to talk about it. Most of the time, the person will ask me a question related to relationships, and instantly God will show me whether they should get the

"I'm just waiting on God" type of answer or tell them my story.

I was able to have a deeper conversation with my mom about everything, as she honestly isn't very receptive to the word I received. We were driving in the car, and she randomly asked me if there was a specific point in time that marked my closer journey with the Lord, and I knew that this was a moment. I explained to my mom that this growth started after dating the person I dated in Grad school. He was the perfect gentleman and very charismatic. His company was right on time for the vulnerable state that I was in. My mom was going through her cancer treatment, and I was taking her to a lot of her appointments, all while working and going to school. It was stressful, and I allowed the brink of my loneliness to open the door to that relationship. Things, of course, didn't go anywhere, but there was never any malicious intent. Just two people trying to make something out of nothing. That relationship is what drove me closer to God. It was the relationship that ended right before I wrote in my journal on June 28, 2015, that I would dedicate my life to God. I was so tired. I was tired of making the same mistakes repeatedly. Through the course of about two months, I began to dive deeper. After telling my mom this story, she said to me, "Well, that is amazing, but do you think maybe God could have been talking about someone else?" Comments like that used to make me angry, but instead, I quietly replied, "No Ma, this is it." She still was very confused but in due time.

This happened with my Aunt Wanda the Sunday I was writing. I felt in my spirit to show her the venue I came across one day. As I showed her this venue, she said to me, "That bridge, the bridge, I have seen it before, that's the bridge." At this point, I am gazing at her in awe. Where in the world has she seen this bridge? I was instantly brought to the revelation I received when walking through the path at my job. I was able to share with her what the Lord showed me about the 69 steps. I realized the song I have always wanted to walk down the aisle talks about taking one step closer, and I let her listen. I have known for over two years that this was the song I wanted to walk down the aisle to.

That next day my dad randomly asked me, "So have you spoken to your friend?" All I could do was laugh and say, God, it is starting to get on my nerves! He looked at me in shock and asked me to explain. I told him how God showed me that certain people should know the intimate parts of this experience, and of course, my dad was a part of that. Thank God my dad already knows a gist, so I didn't have to give too much back story. I explained to him the revelation of the 69 steps, and he was like, "whhhhaaaaaat?" This may be the first conversation my dad and I have had in a little while where he didn't fall asleep on me. I was led to show him the venue, and instantly, it hit me. The Holy Spirit reminded me of a day that I was walking through the trail and thinking. Lord, I know you want me to walk down the aisle this way, but how will people see me at all during the walk? I thought to myself; maybe it should have an elevated area just like the steps that come before the trail at my job. If you recall, my Aunt Wanda spoke of a bridge. The Lord showed me that the two concepts were the same, and instantly I knew. That the place I found had to be the venue. I came across it on May 7th, 2018, and it was NOTHING like what I felt like I wanted, but there was something so special about it.

I have always known that I wanted my wedding to be outside, but because I wanted everything to look vintage, I kept envisioning Victorian-style homes. I kept seeing the home and some type of beautiful garden somewhere near, but as God began to give me the logistics of how He wanted me to walk down the aisle, that idea became less and less realistic. He totally shifted all of that to something different. My colors have even changed, and those of you who know me know my favorite color is pink. I wanted a pretty dusty rose color, something subtle and classy with an accent of burgundy. My color now is rustic blue! Blue! I'm going to say this again, Blue! It definitely isn't what I saw for myself, but it's stunning. I guess that kind of represents this journey. I would have never seen it coming. Seeing how the Lord has been planning my wedding has been fun. It makes me feel so special inside to know He cares. It makes me think about weddings in the Bible. They were very high esteemed events, and why should they not be?! I mean, it is a symbolism of our covenant with God. That's something that should be celebrated. In society, we celebrate, but we never ask God about His part in it. This wedding is being planned with His ideas involved; after all, He is a part of the union.

I remember praying to God that I wanted Him to continue to plan my wedding. This was after I realized He was showing me, my potential bridesmaids. I asked the Lord to financially cover the wedding with his extra bomb resources. My

Papa has the hookup, and as his daughter, I fully plan on partaking. I pray that every soul involved in making my day special will be sent from God and that this day will flow seamlessly. I know this is only the beginning, and the Lord has only shown me bits and pieces. I can only imagine the surprises that are to come. As I wrote in a blog a couple of years ago, the Lord told me there were some things he wanted to give me, but I needed to wait on them. I am beginning to see the trinkets.

"Baby girl, you don't have to reach ....you don't have to do anything extra to get the things that I have set for you....baby I will hand it to you, I will pick it off the highest shelf and give it to you when I feel it's time for you to have it. So sweetie, just stay in daddy's presence, so when it's time, I can find you and give you your gift. I won't have to look for you or wait for you to come back home to me to present your gift, because you will be with me keeping your heart longing for the things of me...I know the plans I have for you baby girl (Jeremiah 29:11), trust that daddy loves you more than anything in this world could ever love you, and I want my princess to be happy. "

—*Papa* 5.7.16

A Union Made for Royalty

During the recent moments of my wait, I have been in such deep thought. When will I see a change, Lord? What do those time frames you showed me really mean? After almost three years, and I get to the month right before August and decide to get so impatient. I realized that it was because my focus shifted. I was doing so much to be at peace, mainly consisting of binge-watching Grey's Anatomy, that it caused me to take my eyes off of the Lord. We all know what happens when you take your eyes off of God from our friend Peter. You sink, and I could literally feel myself doing just that. Something my old friend told me a while ago was to not live off of yesterday's grace. We have moments in our lives when we have amazing breakthroughs in Christ and it's like we want to ride that wave instead of pushing to make one even bigger. Many times I feel like I am fantasizing ALL the time. I know now more than ever who the Lord is showing me my husband is, but when I come down from those clouds, I feel crazy. When I am focusing on what my situation looks like, it feels so much worse.

As I realize the place I'm in, I have made a conscious effort to stay on the course and keep running the race. It's like running a 400 before you become seasoned and know how to run the entire race. You just burst out running as hard as you can, hoping to maintain momentum. It's like I have been running this race, and now I can see the finish line, but I am starting to lose energy. It's that feeling when you can see the finish line in front of you, and you're pushing with everything inside you to get there, but you feel like you aren't moving any faster. You are fighting, only making yourself more tired. I had to check myself and get it together. God has been showing me all these things about our wedding, and I began to talk to him about why he had chosen to show me these things. He said to me, "I am tired of people making my covenant mediocre."

Married couples often talk about how marriage showed them themselves and how marriage is one of the hardest things they ever had to do. By no means am I saying that I think it is a walk in the park but could it be that if you allow God to show you yourself in your singleness, then your spouse will never have to do it? The other day, my dad asked me, "Aria, do you feel you have traits that would be unpleasing to a spouse?" Not knowing where he was going with this, I began to think of things that I had known were not pleasing. Everything I thought of, God had actually been digging out of me. Let it be known that my dad was one of the recipients of my shortcomings, and after my response, he said to me, "The reason I ask is that I honestly couldn't think of anything." I turned to him as I was putting dishes away and told him how much his words meant to me. As a single person at almost 28, people begin to look at you like, what did you do wrong? You're beautiful, driven, successful, and you love God, but you're still single. You must be crazy or something. No one wants to highlight the person you are becoming.

Let's think about this for a second, we are all God's children, and He wants the very best for everyone, right? So what makes you think you deserve the perfect spouse if you have not allowed God to perfect the messed up things in you? During this time, God has been making me a better person. A person that my husband deserves, my children, my family, friends, people whose hearts God will allow me to touch, but most of all, a person that God deserves. God deserves to see me flourish in the essence of who He has created me to be. I have grown to love and cherish that girl. I want you to know that if you have made the Lord our father the captain of your ship then, there will be things that He will have you to work on in you to make you a better person—if you let him. Everyone's story will be different. I don't want you to read my story and desire anything that God is doing in my life. I used to do that, and I would have never even thought of what God was actually doing with my life. No eye has seen, no ear has heard (1 Corinthians 2:9). What I want for you is to desire God's will for your life in all areas. I want you to become the best version of yourself, and as you are doing that, I think you will see God do something special perfectly fit for the king or queen you are.

Lioness Pride

If you recall, there was a chapter title earlier in the book very similar to this one, "A Lioness's Pride." The Bible outlines in much detail what pride is, and it is clear that it is speaking about a boastful kind of pride where someone sets themselves apart from those around them. The Greek dictionary defines the word as exultation and majesty in other translations of the word. Basically, it is a person that sees themselves as the sole reason for success, taking all credit away from God. The pride that describes the dynamics of a group of lions, however, I think has a special significance.

A family of lions is called pride because lions are seen as regal and elevated. I think it is by design that they are one of the few animals that God makes a comparison of Himself to. When you think of the Kingdom of God, it is regal and elevated. As I mentioned before, throughout this journey, I have taken the time to study lions. I felt that if God sees me as a lioness, then I should understand her. As I studied, I began to pick up on their key traits.

Sensei said something to me during one of our many conversations about this journey that wouldn't make sense until now. He said, "You have the power, although your husband will have the authority." I began to explain to him that I totally believe what the Bible says about the order of the household. He stopped me and subtly exclaimed, you can have authority and have no power. Then he asked me, "Who runs the pride of lions?" It is a lioness that essentially sets the tone of the pack and how it will operate. As I began to study and see this for myself, I still couldn't quite locate myself there. I felt I knew where God was trying to take me, but I didn't give myself time to grow. During this time of waiting, God has really shaped and molded me.

I began to duck and dodge the enemy's schemes. Doing this intentionally, made me feel accomplished. I was delighted in the woman I was becoming. I saw myself strong and beautiful; eyes blazing with the passion of purpose. I saw myself letting off the sound of a loud roar, holding a posture of excellence in the eyes of my God. For the very first time, I felt like a lioness of God; strong, eager, adorned, and gracious.

As God slowly gave me the pieces of who I am, He gave me something else that I will always cherish and keep with me until the day I leave this earth. He gave me the pride of lionesses. In the lion kingdom, there is pride that is made up of an average of 3 males and 12 females. In a lion pride, the female lions are the backbone. They are defined by a matriarchy. Webster defines this as a woman who rules or dominates a family, group, or state; specifically: a mother who is head and ruler of her family and descendants. In this, I see my grandmother. I see my family in how the women have created a safety net just with the strength they bring to the foundation of our family; I see myself.

God has given me special women that have made this fight worthwhile. God has given me close friends along the way that have specifically been for the purpose of this journey. Friends whose words have encouraged me to fight the good fight. Women of God who are all pushing for God to prune and fine-tune them into powerful, world-changing women. Women whose words will change lives for generations to come, women who will fight for me, women who will fight for other women. We, as one, bring a certain spice to life.

August...

What did this month mean? At this point, I was going crazy and felt like I had so much on my plate. Let's rewind for a bit because I haven't shared a pretty big present God has given to me. God has given me Unlimited International, Inc. Unlimited is a place where God's children can go to feel his love, fellowship with others, and capitalize off of this thing called life. After bringing this to my brothers Julius and Charmon, they left it up to me to plan, and we have been moving forward since.

In this time, the Lord has given us visions of the bigger picture of Unlimited. We know one day it will be a place where millions will go to receive the undying love of God. Long story short, the responsibility that comes with something like this is real. All the planning and making sure you are equipped spiritually can be taxing when dealing with other life trials.

During August, we made an executive decision to take a break from our bi-weekly meet-ups and do fun outings. All three of us are experiencing different phases in our lives, and we all felt it would be good to take a break. We didn't want to let Unlimited suffer because we were dealing with other things. Working closely with two men can be a headache, regardless of how anointed they are. Side note, ladies, don't think that because your future hubby is a strong man of God, he isn't still a man. I love them so much, but I was starting to feel the weight of planning. I began to feel like I was being overbearing because I wanted things to be done with a specific order. I became angry with what seemed like everything around me. My Aunt Wanda could see it and asked me what was going on. I told her everything, and she said, "You know it isn't supposed to be like this right, you are angry and tired, but why?" I answered all of her questions, and she said, "You are tired because you have taken on some things that God never intended for you to take; give it back!" This put things back into perspective for me, and I felt that I needed a scripture with that principle to take me through. 2 Chronicles 20:15 has been the scripture I have been standing on to keep me balanced in this time. The feeling Ive had since that conversation is a little indifferent. I haven't written very much, and frankly, I've been running from any kind of expectations.

In my times of distress, God has always shown up for me in the sweetest ways. One evening Charmon was speaking on a panel at a church nearby, and I agreed to watch his Goddaughter while he was doing the event. After we went to my brother's place for a little to spend time with his in-laws, who are very much my close family as well. There is nothing like spending time with family when you aren't at your best. Just being in the atmosphere of love can make such a difference. That night as we were leaving the house, I felt myself asking God, when? When will I have my moment? Still feeling my wait was yet to be over. Being patient felt like the worst thing that could ever happen to me. As I stood outside saying goodbyes, I saw a shooting star! Instantly I went, "Whoa!" like a little kid on Christmas when you open the present you had no clue you were getting, but it was more than everything you asked for. It was like God was winking at me, saying, "It's okay, baby, I got you."

A couple of weeks later, I had plans to have dinner with one of my former high school teachers. She wanted to catch up and learn more about Unlimited. This dinner was perfect timing for the place I was in. I knew as we ate I would give her all of the details about Unlimited, but somehow felt we would end up talking about this book. She always sincerely wants to know how people are doing holistically, and because writing this book has been such a big part of my life, I knew there was a possibility. So, of course, as I began to talk about Unlimited, that led to me talking about the blog and then, of course, you guessed it, the book.

As I told her the story, she seemed so captivated. I have to say, out of everyone who I have ever told this story, she was the most engaged. She went on to tell me, "You know you are getting all of these signs because of the calling of the prophetess, right?" I told her I had no idea what that meant until recently. She talked about how God has shown Himself to her all her life, but she has never seen herself as religious. I love this kind of open dialogue because it continues to confirm God's character. I don't see myself as religious either. God also doesn't want us to navigate life religiously (Matthew 23); He hates religion! As we continued to talk, I finished my story with all of the dates. She looked over at me with her head in her hand and said, "You know, today I was thinking that something is happening on the 25th." I felt a jolt rush through my heart. She said, I didn't want to say anything to you, but I just had to. I told her how much I needed to hear that. I told her that I doubted that I would see the Lord move in this month. That night before we parted, she told me to stop doubting and saying maybe something would happen. Begin to say something is going to happen on the 25th. So there I was, a week away from August 25, waiting.

August 25, nothing happened, not a thing. I began to take it as a lesson learned rather than nothing would happen this month. I thought about how God never actually told me anything would happen on the 25th. I got overzealous, and because two other people cosigned, I was all in. I do remember when I started thinking of the 25th and how it didn't quite fit. I thought about how the first time I visited my friend was the 26th, the second time was the 27th, and I couldn't help but feel it would only make sense for God to follow that up with the 28th. Honestly, none of this was revealed to me; I am just guessing trying to put those puzzle pieces where they were never meant to fit and putting God in it.

The enemy was using my intellect and logic to appeal to my emotions just as he did Eve in the garden. God does not move through the logic of our brains but through the Spirit of Truth. There is no second guessing or confusion when He speaks. People's lives can and have been ruined because a prophet put a little bit of their secret sauce into the prophecy. This moment showed me not to move on feelings and emotions and rely solely on God's direction.

I began rationalizing things like, okay, the Lord told me to give him two and a half to three years, and he showed me the six and nine months, but nowhere in there did he say I would see a physical change in this journey. I began to psych myself out about everything, thinking all of this came around so fast but could it be real? It doesn't seem real; maybe I have to struggle a little more. I'm not sure, but I don't feel a feeling of anxiety; I'm just going with the flow. Who knows what will happen this month, maybe nothing will happen at all, but regardless, I have to stay in my lane and keep pushing forward. It would be so easy to fret, but why? It's not going to change anything. Honestly, I feel over it. I want to live my life without thinking of any of this. I feel like I am getting numb to it all. I would like to go a whole day without thinking of this situation. Just block

the thoughts because I know if it is left up to me,
I will find a way to think about him. Just one day!

8.27.18

Today feels interesting. Last night I prayed a prayer that the Lord would guard my mind. I prayed that I would go my entire day without really thinking of any of this. I just feel like I need peace of mind from everything concerning the word the Lord has given me, and I have to say He has honored my prayer. In moments where I find myself going in that direction, my thoughts have quickly deviated; even as I type these words, I feel myself talking about my situation but not thinking about it too hard.

I remember the feeling I had last week going into the weekend. It was the feeling of a much-needed vacation around the corner, the sense of family during the holidays, or big plans with people you love. It was a feeling of excitement for what was to come. I had a feeling that something wonderful would happen. But, more and more, as the time passed, I began to see that it wouldn't. I started to feel a little irrational and started to question things. Could this month pass me by, and there is no physical shift? In most cases, I probably would have felt down or angry inside, but I didn't. The feeling of doubt tried to creep in, and I remembered the questions that people would ask me.

"Are you sure the Lord showed you specifically him?" "He has free will, and people can make their own decisions." "The Lord may have just been showing you the spirit of your husband through him." My answers to all of these what-ifs align with what was shown to me, not my mind. God showed me this numerous times, even when I wasn't trying to see it. Yes, he has free will, but the Lord didn't show me he was my husband so that I could decide whether I wanted him or not. He showed me him because he is my future husband. Remember God didn't show Adam Eve with hopes that he would choose her; He knew the decision Adam would make.

You may draw the notion to your personal experiences and say, "Well, I have gotten word from spiritual leaders about my life, and nothing has ever happened." The thing with this is knowing who is saying what. Is it God, the person, or the enemy? All three are likely, but our word tells us that His sheep know His voice. We know the voice of the Lord can be heard in his word. He will always confirm things through his word.

I have personal experience of this. A couple of years after graduating undergrad I started coaching high school track. At the first track meet, I was running back and forth on the field because I had athletes in field events in two different places. While there I met another coach. As we were conversing, I heard something say, "He is the one." Back then, I wasn't sure where the voice came from, but I knew I wanted to get as far away as humanly possible. I ended up leaving the track meet that day to ensure I wouldn't do or say anything dumb.

I left the meet that day thinking I would never see him again, but I was wrong. We conversed a little more upon our second encounter at another track meet, and he seemed like an incredible person. I don't think I felt anything that denoted him being the one for me during our second conversation. I honestly never really thought of that at all since the initial moment. As time went on, I became very fond of this person and could see myself with him. I always remembered that voice, but it never felt right. Once I began this journey, I realized that the voice I was hearing couldn't have been God. After all, the only thing that was said was "He is the one," which could have meant almost anything. There was never any confirmation from God.

With this notion of August, God never told me that something specific would happen. When the Holy Spirit said to give him this time, I assumed there would be a change when the time was over. I only began to wonder about specific dates when I felt the unction to go back and find an old picture. I have gotten so tired of pushing towards the next hurdle that I don't even care how long it takes. I have been waiting this long what would make the waiting any different from my current everyday life?

I saw my state of mind as an opportunity for me to forget about everything and just walk. I ended my night talking to my mom for a while. She has just finished reading the book up until this point. She shared that she feels like she sees me in a different light. She spoke about the woman I have grown to become.

When you go from everything making sense to nothing, you begin to feel mentally unstable. This entire journey has already felt harsh, and then to come to a point where none of the confirmation you thought you received about something comes true, there is a deep feeling of disappointment. Everything I said before with all these time frames just seems so frivolous. So many times, when I am feeling this way, it makes me feel dumb for being all whiney. I want to see a change. I thought all of what I was feeling was God. The Bible does say our ways are not his ways. So I'm just going to leave this here and move forward.

My mom said something to me the other day that resonated. During this whole process, I have been afraid to live my life a certain way for fear of operating opposite of the way the Lord would have me to. I walk around being afraid of messing up. I have been just trying to keep everything together. I have been holding all these things the Lord has shown me, but as time goes on, I get tired of carrying them, and I'm so tired that I want to drop everything and just breathe. I know after tonight, things will feel weird for me, but I'm done thinking about everything; it just feels like too much. I don't feel angry or weary the way I did before; I just want to live an abundant life.

You begin to feel stupid for holding onto this stuff after a while. Sometimes you just want to give up, but God knows best. God's plan is best, His timing is good. My old friend could very well have a whole girlfriend as we speak, and thinking about a future with her. I'm not going to keep walking around like this. It is time for me to move on and wait and see what happens until the Lord shows me something different.

Butterflies, Rainbows, and Puffy Clouds

8.29.18

I have realized in this time as a person who is called to give the word of the Lord that it's a requirement be led. In moments that you are not confident that it is God, then you wait. Two dates I knew in my head were going to manifest change and nothing. If this were my Abraham and Isaac moment, I guess I would have stabbed my poor baby, like what's going on? Today on August 29, 2018, I feel indifferent. I think I have been waiting for a while now to see a change in this whole thing, and I'm over it. If this Friday passes me by, I can't say I will feel much different than I do today. I find myself asking how the time could go past a certain point?

I feel like that person who knows someone will surprise them, but they keep trying to guess who what when and where. I hate being wrong when it comes to the things of the Lord. When you don't know what's ahead, just stand. I think that's a lesson we can all learn. Even when your heart so relentlessly desires something, don't try to make it happen for yourself when you don't see it. That kind of response, in the long run, will get you hurt. After all of this, it's scary to think about continuing to walk in this same place, but I continue to remind myself that my Father is good; He knows best. God knows what He is doing. I have to trust His timing regardless of what it looks like. I am determined to continue to push forward in life and live it to the fullest regardless of what I see in front of me. When I remind myself of those things, my world aligns again, and I am at peace.

You Sure That's What You Heard?

The other day I was talking to my college best friend to wish her a happy anniversary. Our friendship was rekindled through the writing of this book. It was almost no way I could rehash all of those memories from college and how I met my old friend and not think of her. I asked her if there was a special meaning behind her wedding date, and she explained the trend that fluctuated between 1-3 days and 1-3 years. I couldn't help but think about how special that was, and I know the meaning behind all of that made her secure in her decision to go forward in her marriage. When things are ordained, they are many times out of your control. The number three is divine. I can see how something like that can make a person feel like the father has cosigned on their life decisions. I felt like my opportunity to have a story like that had passed me by.

This time has been so emotionally draining, and no one will understand the inward humiliation that I feel, thinking God was saying something that He didn't say. Following the voice of the Lord takes humbleness. I am reminded that my God is good regardless of what I see.

At this time, my usual inclination would be to walk away, but I want to continue to stick close. The first thing I thought of at this time was never to write again. Still, I find myself jotting down every feeling and emotion with hopes that something will come through. I want someone to see that God will still come through for you even when you look and feel crazy. I love and cherish my God so much, and I can't be angry with Him because He is a good, but I feel very disappointed. I just want my life to be at peace.

August Passed

So here I am today, on September 9th, and nothing. I can't begin to tell you the flood of emotions I have been feeling in these last couple of weeks. It felt like the moment when someone was so sure their significant other would say yes to their proposal, and they didn't. That is the amount of inward humiliation I was feeling. I was so sure I was hearing God. I was so sure that everything lined up, and when I saw nothing, I felt broken and empty. My loneliness was screaming louder than it ever has before. Not lonely because I longed to be with someone but lonely because I felt like God forsook me. Lonely because I was so sure that I was beginning to hear the voice of the Lord, and nothing happened. I was so lost in my thoughts it was challenging to talk to God. For some reason, even though I felt betrayed. I began to feel like I was just coexisting in our relationship.

I felt angry with God. I began to ask questions like, if the time frame I was thinking was wrong, why did you allow me to go on believing something that wasn't true? I even began to convince myself of other possible dates. I kept feeling in my heart that this year couldn't pass. The divine number is three! It is complete in seven! If this year passes, then the impact of the meaning changes for me. I wanted to throw the flash drive I keep this book on out of the window into a lake.

I began to open my mind to allowing people into my life past friendship. I was like a spool of thread just unraveling before my own eyes, and it was tough. All possible dates in my mind had gone away. I almost felt a weight being lifted off of my shoulders. The anticipation is over because the time has come and gone. That in itself helped me to go on day today. Enjoying my work environment also played a huge role in coping. One day as I was headed home from work, I had to take something to my Aunt Wanda. When I arrived, we began to have a conversation, and she gazed at me as I sat on the floor in her room and said, "You're good." Never has she ever said anything like that; at least not before she would ask her famous line, "How's your spirit?" Every time she asks me those questions, I usually really need someone. It's normal for me to keep all of my feelings inside and just deal with them in silence.

She knows that about me, and I know God gives her the unction to reach out when she does because the timing is perfect every time.

I began to tell her how I felt crazy. I explained how I felt everything the Lord was showing me was starting to feel like a lie. If I felt clear about this one thing, then what did all the other confirmations mean? I was disappointed, frustrated, and alone. I didn't want to feel or be close to God, although I knew He would be my only source in this time. I was still reading His word, but there was no intimacy. During this time, I began to see some of the most beautiful clouds. Breathtaking, even better than I mentioned formerly, but I wouldn't enjoy them. I would gaze at them and look away. I couldn't bring myself to engage in the beauty I knew the Lord was showing me until one day, He chased me down with His love.

That afternoon as I was driving to my Aunt Wanda's I saw a breathtaking bundle of clouds stretched out as far as I could see. The clouds were a mixture of white, gray, and a dusky blue, with silver linings everywhere. Before taking in all the beauty, I quickly looked away in disgust as I exited the highway. Little did I know when I made that right turn that they would be right there, God would be right there. As I focused my gaze, I realized it was a different scenery of clouds, and they were beyond beautiful. There was a thick halo of dusky blue stretched across the sky. Underneath were rays of yellow that looked as if the sun was shining right through that strip of the sky. There were dusky blue, white, and yellow clouds everywhere, with random streaks of blue coming down from them. All I could do was laugh. It was like God didn't care that I was pitching a fit about how things were going. He wanted me to know I still love you, baby, I still have My best prepared for you, I still have you right in the palm of My hand.

Still, even after this moment, I went back to feeling the way I did before. I told my Aunt what happened in the moment of my stubbornness on the way to her house, and she thought it was pretty comical. She told me it was like a daughter being upset with her father storming into their dad's house with an attitude, but she knows there is nowhere else to go. She knows she is exactly where she needs to be. My Aunt kept telling me that I was glowing and that she could feel in her spirit that something was different, and in a moment where I won't expect it, I would have a heart of praise. I couldn't see or feel anything she was talking about. She told me I had a look of innocence on my face. She said she could see a change in the woman I was becoming. Words like that have been the most encouraging. When you are grinding and allowing God to change things in you, you often feel invisible. Writing this now reminds me that I talked a lot about not being seen in a previous chapter, and I think this is tying in with something else.

Currently, Unlimited is doing a series called In the Garden. The series has been based on Galatians 5:13-26, the works of the flesh, and fruits of the spirit, with John 15:1-8 as the foundation scripture. After the first night of the series July 6, the next day, the scripture of the day on the YouVersion Bible app was John 15:1-8. Many people messaged the group with confirmations from the message. That same month, we realized a local church was doing a series that spoke about the fruits of the flesh! Not only that, about a month later, one of our favorite pastors, Mike Todd, launched a series called "Planted not Buried," again, the fruits of the spirit. I began to ask, Lord, what are you trying to say to us? This is much bigger than Unlimited. In Mike Todd's series, he talks about how it takes on the look of death when you are planted, but it is the environment God has placed you in to grow. He gave a picture illustration of a seed and its process before you physically see change. The change unseen by the naked eye was so much more significant than the finished product.

I mentioned previously my conversation with aunt Lo about seeds and harvest time. As I have been asking the Holy Spirit what He is trying to show me in this time, I began to see a common ground. There is something special happening in your life when you allow God to be your vinedresser. It's like that moment a bride is getting dressed before the wedding. Everything has to be perfect. Her hair, her nails, her dress, her shoes. No stone left unturned, and no hair out of place. As a bride, you would never run out of your bridal suite half-dressed. As you sit there and allow yourself to get ready, no one sees you. No one sees those late lonely nights you stayed up praying for your husband or wife. No one sees those lonely nights that no matter how much you cried out to God, it seemed like you would never know the day that you would get married. God knew He needed to have you alone to dress you John 15:1-8, He is the dresser.

I think God is showing me that I need to take heart in the growth. Without this time, I wouldn't have become the woman that I am today. Because I felt God showing me something about time frames, I ran out of the dressing room. I ran out prematurely and found myself embarrassed, and ashamed needing to run back to my hiding place. On August 31, I had a conversation with a sweet friend whose much like a little sister, Kimmie, as we were away on a cabin trip. I had already shared the story of the time frame with her, and she agreed with what I felt the Lord was showing me. When the clock struck midnight and nothing happened, my heart felt alone. I opened up to her that night, and she said, just because you didn't see anything physically happening, don't allow that to take away the word God gave you.

You received too many confirmations for it not to be accurate. She said, "You know, as I was riding in the car on the way over here, I was thinking about the six and the nine you spoke about. I thought about how people have something like a gender reveal in a six-month time frame, but the baby hasn't come yet. Something is happening, but you can't see it yet; the baby will be born in nine months. I read a similar revelation like this in a devotional. This was all very encouraging, but after my last go-round with this hopefulness thing, I just can't anymore; it's too disappointing. After my trip to the cabins, the disappointment seemed like too much to bear at times. I felt like I didn't want to even think about anything about the word the Lord had given me. I didn't know how to feel anymore. Where did I do wrong? I was determined not to rethink things because I knew my thoughts would send me off the deep end.

Because of this space, I could feel myself going into a shell about this aspect of my life. As I continued in this space, it had been a while since I spent time with Aunt Lo and Uncle B, so we planned to go to dinner. At dinner, we didn't talk about the space I was in, but before we left, my Aunt mentioned wanting to get an update from the revelation I shared with her. That Sunday, I went to church reluctantly. I haven't felt at home anywhere. During praise and worship, the praise team sang a song where the lyrics said

I know breakthrough is coming,
By faith, I see a miracle,
My God made me a promise,
And it won't stop now.

Seeing those words on the screen made my heart feel full. I wanted to sing those words to the top of my lungs. I even shed a tear, but at some point, I felt like I was singing words I didn't believe. But, I was singing them by faith. As I drove home from church, I reached out to Aunt Lo to see if she was free to chat. I felt ready to vent about everything. As I shared with her all of my doubts and fears, she responded, saying, "You know what God has shown you. It wasn't the devil, and it wasn't you; you know it was God. When God gives us the word, we are called to have faith and believe even when it doesn't make sense. You never know August could have been a powerful month, and just because you didn't see it doesn't mean nothing happened."

Our conversation lasted for almost two hours. She spoke life into me the entire time. It was like a personal church service. When I talk to her, I feel like she knows my heart. She knows what I'm going through, not just from being empathetic but because she has gone through something similar.

As I sit here typing these words, I know that God tells me to trust his process. When God shows me something, I have found myself running away with it, which isn't what his word was designed for. The Bible tells us that his word is to give us hope. I sit here today with somewhat of the feeling I had back in the early summer of 2015, before I ever received a revelation of my future husband. I didn't have a care in the world. All I wanted to do was walk with God. In this moment, all I want is for his will to be done, and although it hurts to think of years passing me by, I know in my heart that if that's God's will, then it is for a purpose. Maybe I can't see it now, but I will realize why later down the road. Faith is not an easy feat, but you will inevitably grow in it when surrounded by a conducive environment.

My Heart

9.24.18

During this journey, many times, I journal my deepest, darkest prayers. Even with this book including so much of my life, I still want parts of my time with God to be private; however, He had a different plan for this journal entry. As the eyes of a young man or woman gaze over these words, even when I have left this earth, I pray the feelings and truth with where I am will help someone struggling.

Lord, this time has been so tough for me. There are some days when I don't know left from right, and I feel so confused. I feel as though I have placed a certain pressure on myself to be perfect in this time for fear that I will disappoint you. That pressure has moments when it builds up, and when certain situations occur, I explode. I have been encouraged to keep walking in this time even though I don't see. I have had vulnerable conversations with people who are very close to me, and they have encouraged me to know that just because I didn't physically see a change doesn't mean you weren't true to your word or I didn't hear you. Yesterday I talked to Tish, and expressed how I have been feeling recently. In our initial conversation, she said she wished it was something she could say to me to help me feel better. We got off the phone, and I told her I would call her back. When we spoke again, she said she wanted to go back to what we were speaking about earlier. When we got off the phone, she prayed and asked God what he would have her say. He said, "Just as he is my child, Aria is my child. If he is not ready, then what kind of father would I be to give her to him prematurely?" She said to me, Aria, I see your side; I know what you are going through, but I don't see what he is going through. We need to be praying for him and what his heart may need. Even if you don't know what to pray, ask God for what he needs and do the same for yourself. Her love is precisely what I have needed in this time.

Lord, lately, I have been angry, disappointed, and frustrated with you. I have been upset with you for allowing me to feel that something would happen in this time, and then it didn't. You knew I wouldn't see anything, but you still allowed me to believe it. Lord, this whole journey has been so trying, but I am encouraged to keep moving with the loving people you have *placed in my life. I am encouraged just to let go. I am inspired to stop walking day to day thinking about this situation. The only thing I am in control of is the way I choose to walk this thing out. A couple of months ago, I prayed earnestly to go at least one day without thinking of this situation, and I honestly feel myself being set up to do that. This isn't mine to handle, and I have given it back over to you. It's like as a young child; my father has a gift for me. It's a diamond, a beautiful diamond. He is still shaping and molding this jewel into the perfect shape for me. I have wanted God to hurry and finish, and He refuses to give His baby girl something He is not done with yet. Would your earthly father give you an uncut diamond (Matthew 7:11)? My God is abundant. He is the God of more than we can ask or think of (Ephesians 3:20). I reminded myself of this when the time was passing me by at the end of August. It was almost like God was showing me. If you can think of it, then that's not it. Even if you think you know, you have no idea what is to come. I am willing to let you be you, God, and I will just be me. Not the Aria who is walking around holding her breath on life thinking that she is helping the situation, but the one who allows her God to be God. I need to walk and know what it looks like to encourage myself in the Lord. I have a feeling I am going to need that tool one day. God, you are so good, and although this journey feels challenging, you never stop showing me how much you love me, and I am forever thankful that...you are my forever love.*

Ari

Why?

My life in the most recent months has been the most significant question mark ever. Why did you even show me this if I wasn't supposed to think about it? Why did you allow me to believe a time frame that wasn't true? I felt everything would line up for me, and then boom...nothing happened, but my disappointment, anger, and frustration.

I went through this time feeling empty and hopeless, not even really wanting to talk to God. I didn't want to turn my back on God and walk entirely away, but I didn't want to talk to him. I remember praying to him, please don't say anything else to me about him. I didn't want anything else from that situation reminding me that I didn't hear God correctly. Lord, I thought for sure I would see a change in August, but I didn't. That also means that the six and the nine are officially null and void, which means that pretty much all of the exciting and unique things I felt the Lord was showing me weren't Him. What if all of it was a lie? Those and many other thoughts were the burning questions in my heart.

I moved from that space with prayer, reading, counsel from loved ones, and the many sermons I watched. I was reminded that even when it looks crazy, God is always moving and working things out in our favor. A recent scripture I have been standing on is Habakkuk 2:3.

For the revelation awaits an appointed time;
it speaks of the end
and will not prove false.
Though it lingers, wait for it;
it will certainly come
and will not delay.

Still, I have had moments of doubt and unbelief, and moments where I could care less if God brings this promise to me. Moments where I see no value in any of this or the person God has shown me. I have thought that if believing all of this feels this bad, I don't want it anymore. After reading this manuscript, my mom said that if God means for this to be, it will be, but in the meantime, you don't be afraid to live your life. I didn't know those words would become so real to me. I spoke to Sensei a couple of weeks ago on a Sunday afternoon when I was grocery shopping. I shared with him all of the emotions of everything that was happening. I told him that I was deciding to move forward. Not because I knew it was what God wanted me to do, but because I was so frustrated. He said to me, "You know that's the trick of the enemy to have you thinking you can't make one wrong turn, or God will take it all away from you." I told him I felt like I was underwater holding my breath, waiting for God to say to me I could come up for air when everything manifested. I realized that I could be Aria. Not the Aria that was waiting for God to manifest His word about a man but just Aria.

Because my motivation was frustration, I found myself in certain moments where I could have compromised my walk, but I am waiting on God's yes before my own. When God said, stay with me, don't leave, He didn't mean to be a hermit; He told me to keep Him near my heart. This new mindset made me feel like a weight was lifted, but there was still some unresolved hurt. Sensei called me not long after our conversation that Sunday to tell me some things the Lord placed on his heart as he prayed for me:

You have been focusing on the wrong things. This whole time all of your focus has been on him. But, so many times, the journey is much bigger than the promise. God has many things for you that you couldn't imagine, but you still have growing to do; there are people out there waiting for you.

Sensei has always been there right when my heart needed him the most. He has been like an angel for sure. We don't talk often, but he always has my back. He listens whenever I need to vent and never judges the place I'm in. I will be forever grateful for his obedience. When we got off the phone, I remember saying, but why? What is the point? Why would you even show me this if knowing him isn't what I need to focus on? What was the end result? I went through my entire day asking that question anytime I thought about this situation. Why Lord, just why?

Today as I approached my day with to-do lists and emails, the question somewhat dissipated, and I didn't care as much about the answer. I had an interview with a student doing a project for a master's program, but other than that, today would be a typical day. One of my coworkers brought the student up and then came back and told me she needed to talk. Once my meeting was over, I went to her office to see what was going on. She said we have a bone to pick with you, referring to another advisor. At the same time, they both said, why didn't you tell us your name was Air-e-ah and not Ar-e-ah!? I could only laugh. The look on their faces made it seem like something much worse. We started having a general conversation, and one of them had to go to a meeting. As my coworker and I continued to talk, we took a walk outside. During that time, she asked me how things were going with dating.

I proceeded to answer with a blanket statement, but for some reason, I felt the unction to tell her about "my story". Before telling her everything, I said, you know this isn't usually something I tell people, but I know when the Lord gives me the floor to do so, and somehow I feel that as I talk to you. I proceeded to tell her the story. She seemed shocked and said to me, you know I felt God was showing me that about a person I was dating prior, and it went so left, so I began to doubt. She thanked me for sharing my story and said it confirmed things for her. She then saw a red cardinal and became excited. She said she feels the presence of her Nana when she sees it. She explained to me how she would always go to her for all advice, and now that she was gone, she sees the bird when she felt like she needed her the most. The cardinal has been an encouragement for me as well. My Aunt Wanda likes cardinals. She says they represent new beginnings. Anytime on this journey when I have felt discouraged or lost, I will see one. Today my friend saw it, it was for her. As I walked back to my office and sat at my desk, He said, *"That's why..."*

The Lioness Den

Today my mom, Aunt Wanda, Aunt Lo, and Sele got together for a lady's brunch. One day Sele and I were on the phone talking about life. As we were conversing, I thought it would be a good idea for her us to get together for brunch. It was such a beautiful fall day spent with beautiful women. When I say beautiful, I don't mean physically attractive; I mean their hearts. Their walks and how the Lord has touched their hearts in different ways have shaped beautiful masterpieces. They are gracious women, and I am so grateful the Lord has blessed me with their presence.

As everyone arrived, I noticed we were all wearing the same colors—a very subtle light dusty rose color, with accents of different shades of blue. I couldn't help but be taken by the fact that everyone was wearing the same colors, except for my mom. She had on black and white. The whole dinner, I kept asking myself the same question, why are we all matching? Where do these colors come from? Then it hit me; they are my wedding colors!

As we were out and about, heading home, my friend from Miami called. It's just something about him that I sometimes feel like I haven't let go of. My whole life, I have loved love. I have always wanted love for myself, and although I don't just fall for every man that has come my way, the ones I fall for always end up hurting me somehow, and honestly, that's a reflection of me. For some reason, I allow men into a space they should have never been granted access. and I pay for it each time. My experiences with these relationships are many times redolent of a familiar place with a different face. All of this is because of my own desires. Thinking of this is disappointing. It's likely why it has been so difficult for me to take my eyes off the person the Lord is showing me. My desire for a relationship has been an idol. I don't want to be this woman. I want to be just as content and happy alone as I would be with a significant other. I don't know what to do to become that woman.

Being in this place makes me feel weak. To live my life looking at and evaluating myself through the lens of a relationship status. As I contemplated these thoughts, I thought about everything in this book, and I felt angry again. Lord, how could you let me believe the time was now. How could it be that I was just walking with you all this time, and then my world was shaken with what you gave me through those steps I took, and look at me now. My faith and my will were all in you, and now I can't see anything. I don't know what's next or if I even heard you correctly to begin with. I am still so hurt and broken from that. My heart aches just to think about it. I don't know what to do and who to be.

As I sit on the side of my bed typing these words, I look over to the book my brother bought me by Lisa Bevere. The same book I put down after reading a passage about a lioness. The Lord told her that He never said she was the lioness but that with her obedience, there would be a lioness that would arise. The book is called Lioness Arising. When my brother bought it for me, he said that all he saw on the cover was Lioness Ari! Reading that book and knowing what God has told me from his mouth that I am a lioness scared me. No way, Lord, were you saying this woman of God Lisa Bevere was called to write a book that I needed to read? This woman has a following of hundreds of thousands of people. How could this girl from Georgia, who no one knows about, be the person this was for? I don't know if any of that is true because clearly, I can get cloudy on God's word, but I felt it deep enough in my soul that I had to stop reading the book.

I have been immersing myself in TV lately so that I don't have to deal with what my heart is feeling, but tonight I want to fight. So today, I think I need to start feeding myself what my spirit needs to be stronger.

All Messed Up

From the last time I wrote, I have come across two revelations that have changed my outlook on life. This entire walk has essentially been full of faith and doubt, but I didn't know what either of them meant. Doubt essentially means to question, and faith means trust.

The Bible tells us not to be double-minded because that person is unstable (James 1:8). The word also tells us not to put our trust in man (Psalm 146:3). Until meeting with Unlimited last Friday, 10.19.18, I didn't realize that I was doing both of those things, and that is precisely why this walk has been so challenging for me.

Many times when we are told when we believe we will receive, we look right at what we believe God for, but God never intended that. Our faith is supposed to be in the promise maker, not the promise. Because my faith was wrapped up in the promise, it always caused me to question everything, but if I had faith in the one true God, my foundation would have been solid. Because my faith was in the wrong thing, I was unstable. This whole book, I am talking about precisely the person. So much so that as I was doing my most recent edits, I felt sick to my stomach. It is outrageous that it took me this long to realize that I was focusing too much on my old friend. After hearing Sensei, Julius, and Uncle B say to me numerous times that I was focusing too much on the person, that this was all about me, it was finally starting to make more sense.

Just recently, God gave Sensei word about that very thing, and I still didn't get it. The Lord promised me something, and all I could do was look straight at it this entire walk. The whole walk, I have been looking at God's hands wanting from him, and not looking into his eyes and being empowered by his love. I guess that's growth. It took me the entire three years since I received the revelation to see this. This is a prime example of how God wants to prune you in specific areas before He can give you certain things. God knew if He gave me what I wanted, I would have never understood what it meant to have true faith in Him. Your faith should always be in Him and not the things that happen around you.

Even with my kicking and screaming, He pushed me. He allowed me to take the steps and make the mistakes, but He didn't give up on where He wanted me. What kind of father would he have been if He had given me something that could have ruined the person He has meant for me to become? Although I still feel lonely, coming to this revelation has changed my whole perspective and allowed me to take my eyes off the promise and trust God completely. I have many moments of deep loneliness, but God has continued to remind me that he is thinking of me, even when it is hard for me to see it.

Last weekend I was riding in the car. I remember asking God a couple of weeks ago, why is it that the rustic blue and dusty rose colors are the colors that began to resonate in my heart? He then showed me the colors I like most in the pictures he paints for me in the sky. This was such a special. "I love you" from God, but for some reason I couldn't really indulge in the moment. Sometimes I wish I was in a place where I could embrace these special moments, but lately, I have been feeling so down.

Begin Again
Grace for His Lioness

I'm not even sure where to start. It has been a while since I have written, well, a couple of months or so. I think I am losing words because I felt things shifting differently, but I was so wrong. I also wanted to go through this book and delete anything I said that had something to do with time specifics. I was feeling crazy and vulnerable all at the same time. But, as I have journeyed through, I have realized that every word I wrote had to stay because, many times, what I did is exactly what we do as believers. We feel God showing us something, and we run with it.

That's what I did. I felt God's spirit, and I completed the story for him instead of allowing him to tell me what was next. I became angry and frustrated, thinking all of this was just a bunch of bull, and I don't know why I ever believed any of it. I rebelled and found myself again compromising. I allowed myself to become more involved with someone I knew wasn't for me and even entertaining thoughts of revisiting my past situations. I fell hard, really hard. I feel that many people in many different circumstances can relate to this place.

Sometimes we try so hard to do what God has called us to do and whenever the thing we are waiting for starts to look crazy and impossible, we throw in the towel. We tell ourselves that life was easier before we started trying to walk in the things of the Lord. This is precisely what I did, but it didn't last long. I had come too far. I just love God so much. I felt myself drifting away but not wanting to be too far from Him. Maybe that was just a result of Him keeping me near. My whole life, I have heard about the grace of God and how it saves us, and never have I experienced what it truly meant until now.

I named my blog Grace to Ari but honestly had no idea why. I remember it coming to me, but it didn't even make sense; it wasn't real to me until now. His grace is all I wanted and needed when I came crawling back to Him after trying to walk away. Angry, frustrated, broken, and hurting, all I wanted was His love. All I wanted was His peace. All I wanted was to feel His presence all over me with no guilt or shame. Without His grace, I couldn't have had that. Without His grace, I would have been left out in the cold to suffer in my condemnation.

As I slowly began to talk to God again, He gave me a vision of how He sees us when we flee from Him when we have sinned—fallen short. He said, "You know how your parents love you, right? They love you regardless of the mistakes you make. They would never kick you out because you have sinned, but regardless because of your state of shame you took your blanket off the bed and decided to lay on the street corner. Thing is your parents never told you to leave, they want you near. They want you to be okay and know that everything will be alright. This is how I see My children when you run away from Me when you have sinned. I never told you, you had to leave. I have always wanted you near to show you how much I love you."

I'm not sure of your family background or structure, but I hope you can see the essence of what God is trying to say here. No matter what you have done, God forgives you and wants you to come to Him. His son died for all sins, not just some. His grace is so sufficient for you if you just let Him in. In this time as I could feel God calling me home. I knew it would be a time of self-reflection. Regardless of if God would continue to take me back, I still knew I needed to address myself. What problem did I have that I involve myself in unhealthy relationships every time something went wrong in life? Was it a false sense of comfort or validation? I didn't know, but I knew I didn't like it and wanted a change.

It wasn't until I came to a revelation of worship through a series by Mike Todd did I realize why my heart continued to reflect the thing that I never truly got rid of, and that's why it would always come out right at the moment where life wasn't going my way.

Time Machine

I'm going to take a moment and reflect on my life as a whole. Growing up, I remembered seeing couples together from all different ages and thinking about how I couldn't wait to have a boyfriend. I started dating my first boyfriend back in high school and lost my virginity during that time. Back then, I had no clue of what was occurring in my heart and soul. I went on to college, and my boyfriend and I broke up during my freshman year. During my time away at school, I dated different people continuing to seek something long-term but not knowing what that meant or entailed. I experienced heartbreak after heartbreak and then wondered what was wrong with me. I would continue to do the same things over and over again. I graduated college a little more mature and a little older but still not understanding life and the spiritual coma I was putting myself in. I went on as my soul reached out for the more spiritual things, but my heart still longed for the very thing that was so important to me even as a child, a companion. As

I gained spiritual knowledge, I began to feel like I could genuinely say I was living life for God. I was putting God first, but the truth is God was only first on that list written down in my journal. Time went on, and the things of God began to sink into my heart a little more, but there was still a void.

In 2015 when I gave up on all love efforts and began to focus my energy on God, I received the revelation of my future husband. I remember feeling so angry because I was there! I was at the point where nothing in this world mattered to me but God. So how then could you tell me something that would essentially cause me to become distracted? Maybe this all was a trick. Perhaps it was a plan to get me to focus on my old friend so much that I would drop the new place God had given me to seek what was being shown.

I honestly can say in my heart that I don't know anymore. I don't know who my husband is, and frankly, I don't care. The thought of it somewhat makes me wince. I spent all this time waiting for someone who could care less about me. I learned from Pastor Todd's series that we say we love God, but we have not made Him the captain of our ship, and that is why we find ourselves sinning against him. I realized that love and companionship was the captain of my ship. I was willing to compromise where I was if the price was right. Not that I instantly would run away from God, but the enemy knew what it took to chip away at me until I would break, but God. God knew that He would always be there to rescue me when it was too much for me to bear.

I remember crying to my Aunt Wanda one lonely night when I was all of about 22 or so and saying to her, "It feels like everyone gets snatched away!" I cannot tell you how many men I have found myself wanting to be with, and they moved, or I did. Now I know what I thought was just happenstance was God. That was God giving me my way out because He knew I had no clue what or why I was doing the things I was doing. Pastor Todd's series on worship spoke about how worship is more than a song. We worship God by showing him a love for the grace He has given us. We honor him in our entire being. Knowing that I had an idol of relationships sitting on the throne of my heart all this time in the place of the one who adorns me almost brings me to tears. God loves me so much that He watched me all these years as I have stumbled through life trying to find my way, and He just stuck with me. It was like He was there with me the whole time, waiting

to say, it's okay, baby girl, I know you don't understand it now, but you will. Until you see clearly, I will be here, I'm waiting for you.

Today I know that when we worship God, we do so with the center of our being. We do so with our thoughts and our will because without His grace; we are nothing. Without His grace, death would be the outcome. God loved me so much He sent Jesus, Yeshua, The One True King to be sentenced to death so I can call him mine. I am free because He lives in me. That sacrifice was everything. It is the culmination of our faith.

For the first time in my life, I truly feel the sentiment of God not needing to do another thing in my life, because of what He has already done. His grace is why I am. His grace is sufficient for all things. Mike Todd said something in his series that stuck with me. He explained how as believers, we don't know what the word worship means, and because of that, we have gone most of our lives not worshiping God.

Worship is a holistic term in that we worship God with our entire existence. Everything we do behind the scenes and on stage represents what is in our hearts. Understanding this made so many scriptures in the Bible make so much more sense. There are so many scriptures in the Bible that speak about not worshiping two masters. I remember thinking when I would read that, but God, I would never just sing songs to satin or practice satanic things; I could never worship satin. Little did I know, I have. If my actions were to reflect who I was worshiping, it wasn't God. I never even realized this. I wasn't by any means intentionally going against God's will, but the times that I found myself angry with God, I was walking away from him in my heart. It was wrong for me to see God in this light. God would never do anything to harm me. Whenever life looked crazy, I should have never set my heart to feel God wants anything but the best for my life.

Instead in those moments, the lies of the enemy became appealing, and I began to compromise in my heart. Before I knew it, I was falling. If we put God in the captain seat of our hearts and realize He is always in control, the issues of life will never feel the same again. Not that they won't come because they will but knowing that you have the Almighty one on your side, you should feel invincible. Satan deserves no place in your heart. Nothing deserves the main seat of your heart but God. Pastor Todd says God is the only One who can afford to be there, He paid the cost through the death of His only Son. Nothing else in this world could pay for what it costs to have our hearts, so why would we give it away to someone who wants to destroy it?

That understanding should make you run from sin. I know I will always find myself asking for forgiveness for mistakes I will make in life. I will probably always have to remind myself that nothing and no one deserves the seat that God sits on in my life because as long as you are living and breathing, the enemy wants you dead. This time of my life has been the most confusing and enlightening all at the same time. I don't know what's next or if this book that I thought would be so impactful will even make sense anymore. I feel pride wouldn't let me publish a book about a man I never married, but maybe it's not about that. Perhaps it's about the mistakes we make as young women and the journey it takes us through as we navigate the voice of God to His promises.

When I think of God's promise and my old friend, the only thing I hear is him telling me was he wanted to explore things with another young lady. All I can think about is that he doesn't answer my calls and responds through nonchalant texts. I think about how I wasted three years focusing on the manifestation of something that has made me look like a fool. As I sat and watched the cursor blink and thought of how to end this chapter, the first thing that came to mind was, I will wait and see, but I won't. I'm not going to wait and see; I am going to walk and see the things God has for my life right now! I want an abundance of the things I need to see right now and in this moment and the essence of each particular day after. Whatever day belongs to the manifestation of this story will come, but until then, I will focus on what matters in life.

"And out of the wilderness came the Lioness."

8.21.21

The Beginning...

Epilogue

The Rose in the Desert
Holy Spirit Inspired by Sheldon Peterson (Sensei)
10.13.17

Behold the rose that grew in the desert, yet no one saw. It blossomed in the heat, yet no one noticed. It grew with a lack of water, yet no one saw. It grew despite the heat and scorching wind, yet no one saw. Not why, but how is the question, how can something grow without proper nutrition? Was there someone that came and fed it when we weren't looking? That would simply be impossible, for distance is overwhelming.

Yet it continues to grow, flourishes in the heat; it continues to thrive despite the misery. The Lord says—when no one sees I do, when no one appreciates you, remember it was the same for Christ too. I know the greatness that beats inside you; I see it because I placed it there. I know the birthplace of your potential; I know it because I created all of its essentials. I love you even though no one sees you; I love you even though sometimes they undervalue you.

You see, you're the rose that no one notices; you're the rose that grew from beneath. You're the rose that they never saw coming, yet you're the rose that everyone will want in their kitchen. And when your time comes, many will act as though they were there but remember no one saw, so only the Lord can claim that He was there. So for now, your greatness will remain a secret, for many times, you shall go unnoticed. But as a time came when Christ was a secret no more, a time will come when you will be the rose that everyone claims they saw.

8.5.21

To the Rose that grew, but no one understood how it blossomed or how it bloomed.

To the lioness of God,

My friend, and Sister on this journey. Your growth is a direct indication of the presence of God in your life. You will blossom and you will bloom wherever you are planted because God deemed it so!

Love,

About the Author

Aria Gaines, acclaimed writer, author, and entrepreneur. A true Atlanta Native. She has embodied a proclivity for journaling and reading since early childhood; however, her passion for sport has inspired many of her life endeavors. She describes her writing journey as "The dream I could have never dreamed of". She is the CEO of a non-profit organization Unlimited International Inc., where she strives to empower others to be all they aspire to be in every aspect of life. For more information visit gracetoari.com | Instagram: @ariyejide

www.ingramcontent.com/pod-product-compliance
Lightning Source LLC
Chambersburg PA
CBHW011801090426
42811CB00008B/1011